MERCEDES-BENZ 300 SL

With photography by René Staud,
text by Jürgen Lewandowski

teNeues

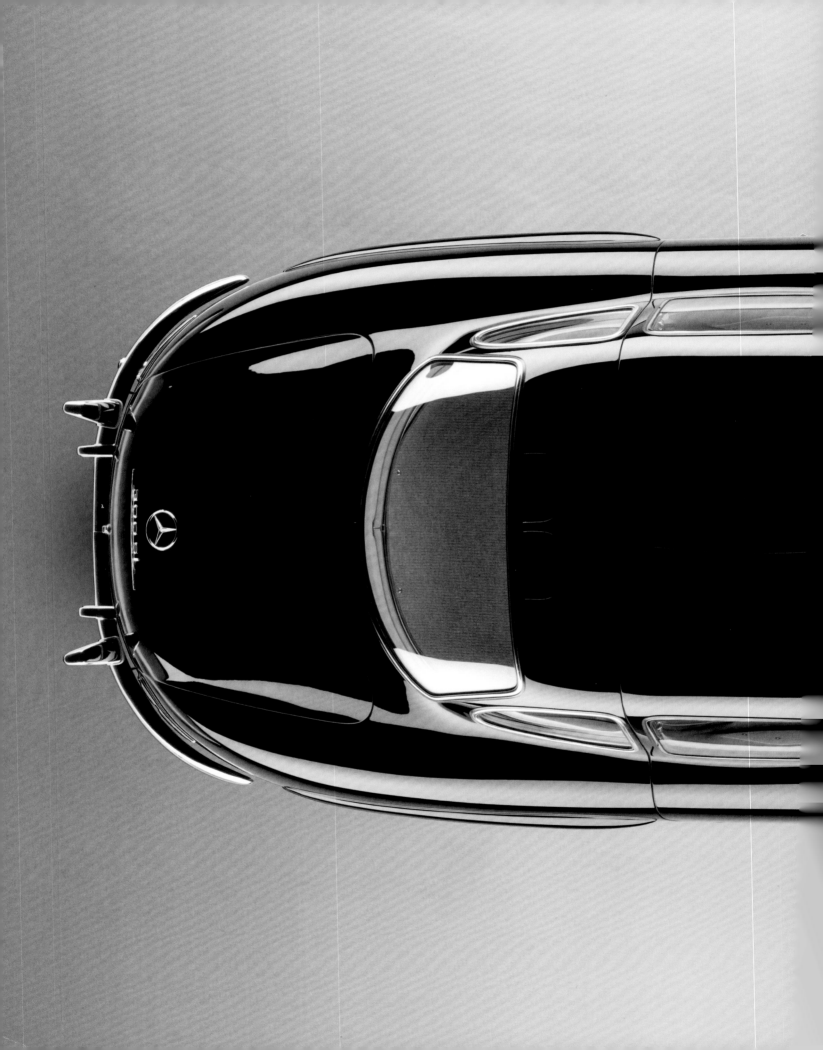

Upward-opening gull-wing doors made the 300 SL coupé a legend,
but the wingless roadster also became an icon in its own right.

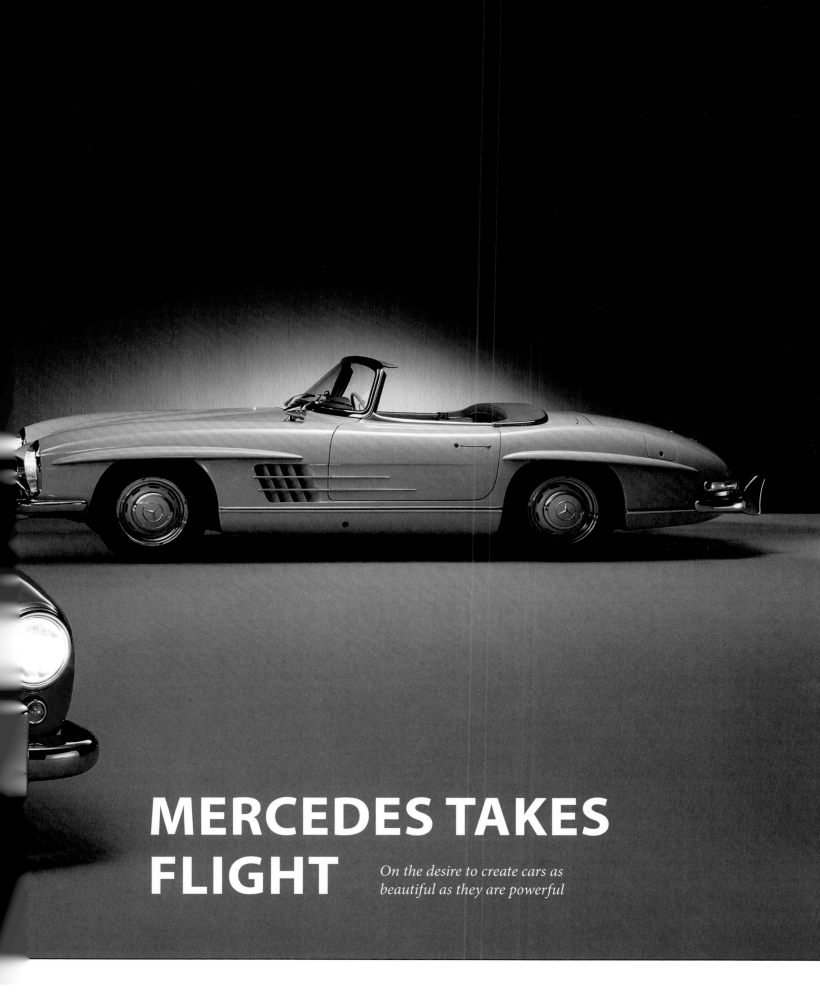

MERCEDES TAKES FLIGHT

*On the desire to create cars as
beautiful as they are powerful*

In this 300 SL, now perfectly restored, Hermann Lang and
Erwin Grupp finished second at the Carrera Panamericana
in Mexico in 1952.

By the 1930s, were there any glamorous sports cars for people who had made it? Cars for promenading on the world's boulevards, for posing in Biarritz, on Long Island, or along the Kurfürstendamm? It was not until that decade that the automotive industry discovered this significant market niche, a new evolutionary stage in mobility. While the 1920s were shaped by hedonism, the car still played a minor role in this lifestyle. What's more, after the big financial crash, it was not until the 1930s that people had much money again. In addition to the development of ever more powerful engines, manufacturers of luxury vehicles then discovered design as a selling point.

1886

The birth of the automobile:
Carl Benz applies for a patent for his
"vehicle powered by a gas engine"
on January 29. That same year, Gottlieb
Daimler introduces the motor coach.

1900

In the name of his daughter: Emil Jellinek, a
distributor of Daimler Motoren Gesellschaft
vehicles, introduces the "Daimler-Mercedes"
label for the newly developed engine,
named after his daughter.

1926

Forces combined: In June, Daimler
Motoren Gesellschaft and Benz & Cie.
merge to form Daimler-Benz AG,
with its head office in the district
of Untertürkheim in Stuttgart.

PIONEERING WORK

Without a doubt, Mercedes-Benz, the oldest automaker in the world, is one of the most important pioneers of all time. Not only did it make the automobile run, it also devoted great zeal and passion to the further development of this world-shaking invention. One milestone was the development of compressor models at Daimler by Ferdinand Porsche, Head of the Engineering Office and member of the board at Daimler Motoren Gesellschaft from April 1923 to 1928. After merging with Benz, the new company Mercedes-Benz offered extraordinarily powerful vehicles, including the Mercedes 24/100/140 PS designed by Porsche in 1924 (later the Mercedes-Benz Type 630) and the sports car models of Types S, SS and SSK available from 1926 onward. They would dominate racetracks in the coming years and win important races such as the Mille Miglia in Italy and the Tourist Trophy in the United Kingdom in the hands of drivers like Rudolf Caracciola. The high point of this series was the SSKL, only used by the factory, that delivered 300 metric HP with an activated compressor.

Mercedes-Benz gained a lot of knowledge from these expensive, race-tested models, of which about 300 units were built altogether—knowledge that benefited the 500 K, introduced in February 1934. The in-line six-cylinder engine of its predecessor was now an in-line eight cylinder with five liter displacement and 100 metric HP, which jumped to 160 metric horsepower with an activated compressor. The 540 K with 5.4 liter displacement and 115 (180) metric HP followed in October 1936, while only a few prototypes of the 580 K planned for 1940 were ever created.

Thanks to these compressor vehicles, for the first time, Mercedes-Benz had a glamorous car in its range. A few trailblazing body designs meant that the car was more than just a means of transportation. Film stars and industrialists alike accessorized with this spectacular special roadster—the automobile had finally been discovered as an object of a luxurious life. Of course, these vehicles could also get you from A to B—but now, how you traveled also played a key role.

1928

Representative fleet: Under the new brand name Mercedes-Benz, the portfolio consists of four mid-class and upper-class models, Types 630, S, SS, and SSK.

1934–1940

Powerful compressors: Types 500 K, 540 K, and 580 K achieve up to 200 metric HP with their eight-cylinder engines.

1946

Reconstruction after the war: On January 3, the occupying Americans grant Daimler-Benz permission for new, though limited, production.

Knowing this back story is important in grasping the sensation the appearance of the 300 SL caused, from the early 50s up to today. But this wasn't the plan at all: At the start of the 1950s, Mercedes-Benz was simply looking for an opportunity to carry on the legendary race victories of the Silver Arrows, which had earned the automaker the reputation of being nearly unbeatable in motor sports. But there were problems: The Americans—Stuttgart was in the American sector of a country divided by the four victorious powers—only approved the construction of a single model for the brand with the star: the 170V. And it was only to be built as flatbed truck, van, and ambulance—and in lacking or destroyed production plants, with a non-existent tool industry, constant power failures, and nearly unavailable raw materials.

EVOLUTIONARY STAGE: TYPE 300

In light of these facts, the meeting which General Director Wilhelm Haspel called for his board of directors in December 1947 could definitely be called unusual. The only thing Haspel discussed with his colleagues was the planning of a sports car or presentation car which would draw on the fame of the large compressor models. Though everyone present understood that Germany would likely only accept a few models for a long time to come, there were interesting markets globally, such as the US, South America, or even Switzerland, where a variety of American and European manufacturers were already doing good business. Furthermore, this sort of model would also promote the company's image and convey the old renown to the present era.

1947

Presentation car: In December,
General Director Wilhelm Haspel holds
a meeting and reveals the plan for
a successor to the successful
compressor models.

1951

Adenauer's Mercedes: The Mercedes 300
is presented at the International
Motor Show in April, and the first
West German chancellor later makes
it the official state car.

1951

Sports car decree:
The board decides to build
a sports car on June 15—
the starting signal for the
development of the 300 SL.

The holy grail and forgotten SL: A look into the cockpit of this 300 SLR is truly one of a kind—it is the 300 SL proto- type for the 1953 season, and it was never used.

One of the directors argued for the construction of a large sedan and a large sports car—in his plea, Dr.-Ing. (Graduate Engineer) Otto Hoppe invoked the great tradition of the past which Mercedes-Benz was to build on. When Max Wagner, another member at the table, came forward as an opponent of this project, regarding it as still much too early for such thoughts, Wilhelm Haspel said, "Mr. Wagner has no real heart for the big car." However, he wanted "to have a leader, a representative vehicle that is in keeping with our tradition."

The result of these deliberations, the Type 300, was presented to its first admirers at a motor show in April 1951—and from November 1951 on, the 300 was also showcased at dealerships. No fewer than 4778 units of the W 186 I—the internal designation of the large sedan—were built up until March 1954, when it was replaced by the 300 b. The new "big" Mercedes was large, heavy, and solid, but it had a displacement that could be built upon to keep up with the competition—and so, slowly, the desire and willingness to enter a sports car in major races and revamp the sporting reputation of the automaker grew.

1952

Motor sports debut in Italy: In its first race, the 300 SL takes second and fourth place at the Mille Miglia on May 3 and 4.

1952

Triple victory: Karl Kling takes the sports car prize in Berne on May 18, beating Hermann Lang and Fritz Riess. Racing legend Rudolf Caracciola drops out after an accident and ends his career.

1952

Double victory: Hermann Lang and passenger Fritz Riess finish ahead of Helfrich and Niedermayr at the 24 Hours of Le Mans on June 14/15.

La Aurora International Airport in Guatemala: A W 198 I poses for comparison with the gull-wing doors of a transport aircraft in 1956. This was the first 300 SL transported by air—imported from Panama to Guatemala.

1952

Absolute dominance: The 300 SL takes the first four places at the big sports car competition on the Nürburgring on August 3: Lang ahead of Kling, Riess, and Helfrich.

1952

The fourth victory in five races: Kling/Klenk win against Lang/Grupp at the Carrera Panamericana from November 19 to 23, setting a new track record.

1953

The missing link: While it was never used in motor sports, this prototype represents a further development of the 1952 race car on the journey to becoming the series-production 300 SL.

These initial considerations were used to create the designation of a car yet to be developed: a sporty, lightweight 300—in other words, the 300 SL.

LABOR PAINS

On June 15, 1951, the board agreed to build a sports car, paraphrased as a "special design of Types W 187 (220) and W 188 (300 S)." At the end of June, a meeting was held in the central engineering department. Head engineer Rudolf Uhlenhaut told his employees Franz Roller, Ludwig Kraus, and Manfred Lorscheidt what key specifications the new sports car had to meet; then, Hermann Lang, Karl Kling, and Alfred Neubauer reported what drivers and the racing department expected of this model, defining the initial parameters.

The first problems were already apparent here: the 300, which had been selected as the basis for the design, was a sturdy sedan from its very basic concept, whose in-line six-cylinder engine output 115 metric HP. And, as is to be expected in this era, the stability and simplicity, low noise level, and limited wear values of pure metal were preferred when designing the engine over the low weight of aluminum—the completed engine weighed no less than 584 pounds (265 kilograms).

It is no wonder that Neubauer fought tooth and nail against it. According to various reports and stories, for a long time, Neubauer made critical comments about nearly every detail, continuously demanding more power and a lower weight. Then the standard transmission of the 300 was not good enough for him; he complained about the quality of the brakes and the tire diameter. In short, he would have seriously jeopardized the project if Fritz Nallinger, Head of Engineering, Development and Testing, had not impressed upon him that there was no alternative—and that the board would quickly bury the SL if they caught wind of Neubauer's doubts.

1954

A star is born:
The Mercedes-Benz 300 SL is presented at the International Motor Sports Show in New York from February 6 to 14.

1954

The legacy of a legend: In the spring, the development phase for a successor to the 1952 race car is started. The 300 SLR is set to go to the starting line at sports car races the next year.

1954

Series production: Initiated by US importer Max Hoffman, delivery of the 300 SL series-production model begins in August.

The big day: On February 14, 1954, the 300 SL celebrates its world premiere at the International Motor Sports Show in New York, along with the 190 SL behind it. In Germany, the 300 SL costs just under 29,000 German marks.

Max "Maxie" Hoffman had imported Volvo vehicles to Vienna, then fled to the US in the 1930s. There, he specialized in the sale of European luxury cars—including the 300 SL.

1954/55

The return of the Silver Arrows: Juan Manuel Fangio wins twice in a row at the Formula 1 World Championship or its predecessor in the W 196 (on which the 300 SLR is based).

1955

The Uhlenhaut Coupé: Two coupés are created based on the 300 SLR race car that pass from the ownership of Head Engineer Rudolf Uhlenhaut and into automobile history.

1955

The tragedy: At the 24-hour race in Le Mans, a collision with 300 SLR driver Pierre Levegh causes one of the worst accidents in motor sports history, resulting in 84 deaths.

In the US, the car with the "Flügeltüren" is christened the Gullwing. Importer Max Hoffman increased sales figures for all Mercedes models from 253 to 6048 in the years from 1952 until 1957.

MYTH-MAKING: PART I & II

What followed was a prime example of creative problem solving, or in other words, myth-making part I. Despite, or in part even because of, the limitations of the time, such as existing regulations and technical requirements, the 300 SL was an automobile that would become an absolute legend. Details are described in the "Design" and "Innovation" chapters. But, in brief: The in-line six-cylinder engine was modified to increase its power. The chassis was designed to be as good—and, importantly, as light-weight—as possible, using all the tricks they could muster. The tubular frame introduced by Rudolf Uhlenhaut and dramatic gull-wing doors not only delivered the desired improvements, but also ensured that, in compari-

---

1955

Bittersweet triumph: Despite the Le Mans tragedy, the 300 SLR still wins a world championship. Stirling Moss earns this distinction at the Targa Florio on October 16.

1957

Finale for the Gullwing: The production of the 300 SL coupé with the dramatic gull-wing doors is discontinued in order to make space for the roadster.

1957

Long live the 300 SL roadster: The roadster, which is designed to satisfy US buyers' desire for more comfort, celebrates its premiere at the Geneva Motor Show in March.

son to proper race cars, the 300 SL would become an unusually refined vehicle.

It is not surprising that the racing sports car attracted attention when it appeared on the starting line in early 1952—for Mercedes, the first time in this category since the war. Although Alfred Neubauer tried to integrate more power, lower weight,

and larger tires in the car up to the very end ("The press and public in Germany expect an overall win from a Mercedes sports car in my hands"), he came to terms with the car. He would rather compete with this vehicle than not compete at all. Thus, the path was clear for a racing success story, or myth-making part II. Many small parts work together to ensure an

1961

Fans of the Gullwing: The Gull Wing Group International is founded in San Francisco. Number of founding members: 18.

1963

The end of an era: After 1858 units built, production of the Mercedes 300 SL roadster is discontinued.

1963–1971

Successor 1: As a direct descendant, the 230 SL (starting in 1967/68: 250 SL and 280 SL) appears on the scene. Due to the shape of its roof, it is nicknamed the "Pagoda."

The first 300 SLs were delivered with two-spoke steering wheels—from today's point of view, a safety risk in case of frontal collisions. The car known as the Uhlenhaut Coupé from 1955 already had a steering wheel with four spokes.

automobile rises to the level of an icon—the help of a cult film here, a photo with a celebrity there. But with the 300 SL, the design and its motor sports history are clearly first and foremost. The latter is even more notable given that four wins in five races in the year 1952 were enough to achieve it.

THE FORGOTTEN STAR

To find the link between the race car from 1952 and the series production model from 1954, you must dive deep into the documentation of the Mercedes-Benz archive. After some digging, you will find a special 300 SL, with which the automakers from Stuttgart could have been able to secure victories in 1953.

However, it was decommissioned, its entry in Formula 1 sacrificed before it could show off its new injection engine and 230 metric HP.

The success of 1952 did cause Mercedes to think again about entering a few races the following year, which was contrary to the original plan. Ultimately, however, the decision of the board was upheld; the company would instead dedicate all its efforts to the development of the Grand Prix race car for 1954. Not the worst decision, considering Juan Manuel Fangio still won two World Championships in his first attempt with a revived Silver Arrow.

1971–1989

Successor 2: The next generation, the R 107, looks more angular than its predecessor but remains true to the legacy of the 300 SL.

1989–2001

Into the new millennium: The R 129 features new technology and an attractive exterior, and is awarded the international "Car Design Award."

2001–2012

Fresh air at the push of a button: The Vario roof of the R 230 can be opened or closed in 16 seconds, to the delight of 169,434 buyers.

The history of the 300 SL is not complete without the Uhlenhaut Coupé. Head Engineer and later board member Rudolf Uhlenhaut drove this car personally. Today, the 300 SLR coupé rests in the Mercedes-Benz Museum in Stuttgart, with the Grand Prix eight-cylinder engine under its long hood.

All the same, work on the further development of the model that had such a successful racing season had already begun in 1952. Rudolf Uhlenhaut summarized the need for improvement as follows: "Lowering the power requirement of the vehicle and improving road-holding is just as important as increasing the power." Specifically, the weight, center of gravity, braking power, and engine—particularly injection—had to be honed.

READY FOR SERIES PRODUCTION

Although no race car was to be used in 1953, a vehicle was created that implemented many of Uhlenhaut's recommendations—this model, with vehicle identification number W 194 011 and approval number AW 24-6303, was equipped with many elements that were then adopted in the "series" 300 SL.

The 1953 prototype designed in keeping with Uhlenhaut's ideas had a wider, flatter front section, larger gull-wing doors that were drawn further forward, a lower roof line, and dramatic vent slots in front of the doors and in the rear fender—but its real surprise was under the hood. The M-198 engine with fuel injection now supplied 225 metric HP at 6000 rpm. In the first test drives, the new member of the racing team, Hans Herrmann, achieved a new lap record on his first go around the Solitude racetrack in Stuttgart.

2003–2009

Reminiscence: The super-sports car Mercedes-Benz SLR McLaren appears in 2009, as well as the special edition SLR Stirling Moss— limited to 75 units.

2009

The return of the gull-wing doors: 52 years after the end of the 300 SL coupé, the SLS AMG picks up on this dramatic element once again.

2013

SL goes electric: The SLS AMG Electric Drive is introduced to the market, featuring an electric drive and technology from Formula One.

A critical point in the development of the 300 SL was the double-win at the Carrera Panamericana in November 1952. A vehicle with the characteristics of the 1953 prototype would have surely won on the racetrack, but the car suddenly had a new purpose. After the victory at the Carrera Panamericana, the US market discovered vehicles from Daimler-Benz. Importer Max Hoffman suggested the Stuttgart automaker build a road vehicle from the successful race car for his rich clientèle. For this transformation, an injection engine was integrated, while the significantly improved chassis was omitted on instructions from the accountants they had back then, too—a confounding choice to this very day. On the other hand, they had agreed on a sales price of 29,000 German marks and wanted to steer clear of the territory of the 34,500 German mark 300 Sc coupé. Despite this, the development of the 300 SL was a triumph.

BIG IN AMERICA

Preparations for the presentation of the series-production 300 SL began in the spring of 1953. It celebrated its world premiere at the International Motor Sports Show in New York, which took place from February 6 to 14, 1954. For the first time,

the 300 SL and 190 SL were exposed to the critical gaze of the public. Having the premiere in the US was a testament to Hoffman's influence, but also a sign of the management's strategy: "Germany and Europe were so poor at the time that we hardly imagined the 300 SL could also be sold in our country," Heinz Hoppe said about the price of the 300 SL. "We were asking twice the price of a Corvette or Jaguar—only Ferraris were comparably expensive."

Indeed, the US was the country where the 300 SL sold in the greatest quantities: About 80 percent of the 1400 gull-winged cars built and about 70 percent of the 1858 roadsters ultimately ended up in the US. Seeking a catchy translation for the car's doors, "Flügeltüren" in German, the Americans instinctively and poetically compared the feature to the wings of a seagull and coined the term "gullwing." The synecdochical name is also fitting because it was ultimately the gull-wings that helped the 300 SL take off.

The 300 SL was able to be brought to series maturity in just a few months while the development department was focusing primarily on building the new Formula 1 vehicles for a simple reason: the most important components were already on hand. The W 194 (i.e. the single unit from 1953) was taken as the visual basis, as was the injection engine from this car. For reasons of cost, the refined chassis was omitted and the vehicle was left with the W 194 technology from 1952.

The first units were shipped starting in August 1954; there were to be 146 that year. In both assessments from contemporaries as well as from a modern perspective, the 300 SL was a sensa-tion. The car generated enthusiasm from day one and fascinated all who saw it. As American industry periodical *Road & Track* wrote after an initial test, "If a comfortable interior accompanies remarkably good driving characteristics, with almost uncanny road-holding ability of the wheels, smooth and precise steering, and an output that comes close to the best cars of the day, and may even surpass them, there's just one thing left to say: The sports car of the future has become a reality."

ONE FOR THE ROAD

At the request of sun-drenched Americans, the American road-ster followed in 1957. It is hard to understand today why it replaced the 300 SL coupé, the production of which ceased in the same year. As Heinz Hoppe, then Head of Mercedes-Benz of America, remembers, "The greater part of production went to the US, and Max Hoffman continuously reiterated the belief that his spoiled public would appreciate a little more comfort, a little more trunk space, a little more fresh air."

The fact is that only 76 coupés were shipped in 1957—but 554 roadsters had found their way to customers. Few manufac-turers have shown the courage to take a legend at the height of its fame off the production lines—but perhaps the abrupt discontinuation of coupé production after 1400 units is another puzzle piece in the legend of this car.

The roadster celebrated its premiere at the Geneva Motor Show in the spring of 1957. In order to make the desire for more com-fort a reality, the dramatic gull-wing doors on the car needed to give way to "proper" doors. Since the previously used tubular

Photographic homage to a masterpiece:
The Uhlenhaut Coupé in front of a stylized
initial, staged by René Staud

frame was too wide to create the front-hinged doors now required, the delicate frame was modified accordingly.

The roadster was the more comfortable and practical 300 SL. The fabric top could be lowered under a fixed fairing in just a few easy steps; those who wanted a little more comfort in the wintertime could have a hardtop installed. The in-line six-cylinder engine continued to roar and, in the sunshine under blue skies, it could now be heard better than ever. What's more, the heat masses pumped out by the engine no longer had such a sweat-inducing effect—when traveling in the summer, the roadster was definitely the more sensible car.

THE HOLY GRAIL

No history of the 300 SL is complete without mentioning the car known as the Uhlenhaut Coupé. Only two units were ever made—and they were only driven by the boss himself.

In the spring of 1955, the W 196—which was driven in 14 Formula 1 races in 1954/55, winning eleven of them—also appeared at races in the World Sportscar Championship in a slightly modified form. The W 196 R (for race car) became the W 196 S (for sports car), though it officially bore the designation 300 SLR. The technology of the two models was nearly identical—the automakers in Stuttgart simply enlarged the displacement of the SLR to three liters.

Rudolf Uhlenhaut had two of the ten total W 196 S models built with the coupé body, the appearance of which was closely based on the series-production model. However, it had become even more perfect and beautiful than its role model. Naturally, the cars with vehicle identification numbers 0007/55 and 0008/55, today both in the possession of the Mercedes-Benz Museum, had an in-line eight-cylinder engine with an output of 302 metric HP. This power and performance was unmistakably heralded by two short exhaust pipes in front of the passenger door which opened right into open air.

Since Mercedes had withdrawn from motor sports after the accident at Le Mans in 1955, both of Uhlenhaut's coupés remained "private sedans, his toys," as motor sports legend Stirling Moss said, who witnessed how the head engineer regularly appeared at the racetrack with these cars. Uhlenhaut must have taken great pleasure in the vehicles, as his employees long remembered how the boss would drove his coupé across Stuttgart to get to work in all weather conditions. Thanks to the noise this car made, the head engineer's arrival was always announced from a great distance away.

The 300 SLR coupé is the pinnacle of what the Stuttgart automakers meant by a "sporty, light-weight race car." To this day, it is still the non plus ultra of all Gullwing models, a sort of holy grail.

Photographic homage II: The Uhlenhaut Coupé and its perfectly illuminated stylistic lines. When Rudolf Uhlenhaut drove his 300 SLR to the Grand Prix races, the large mufflers on the two hefty exhaust pipes covered at least the worst of the noise.

Kienle Automobiltechnik in Heimerdingen, Germany, calls itself the world's largest restorer of
Mercedes classics independent of Daimler AG. After careful treatment, this 300 SL shines.

Still rough and unpolished—the 300 SL
from 1953 was a true race car.

FORM FOLLOWS FUNCTION

On the art of transforming technical necessity into creative variety

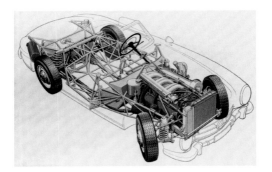

It is not an icon in the classic design sense, but the beau from Sindelfingen nevertheless has a special spot in the parkorama of automotive design." There is hardly a better or more precise description than that from Paolo Tumminelli, professor at the Köln International School of Design with a research focus on automobility. The 300 SL is certainly not a vehicle from the drawing board of a luminary like Flaminio Bertoni (Citroën DS) or Giovanni Michelotti (Maserati Sebring). Instead, it grew from necessity into the "sports car of the century."

Originally, in the early 1950s, the sought-after sports car from Mercedes was supposed to be based on the 300 sedan. In order to give it a boost in terms of power technology, Head Engineer

Rudolf Uhlenhaut added two ingenious ideas: the tubular frame and the gull-wing doors. With these solutions, the 300 SL personified the design principle of form following function in the best possible sense.

Critical points during the initial design phase of the car included the chassis and body. The vehicle was to be as lightweight as possible. The vehicle frame needed to be bend-resistant and torsionally rigid in order to absorb the acceleration and braking forces. The most advantageous design was just a tubular frame in which tubes have to absorb the tensile and compressive forces. A comparison with the tubular ladder frame of the pre-war W 154 race car provided a reference point for the excellent rigidity. Both feature the same resistance to warping, but at 110 pounds

The delicate tubular frame was light-weight and rigid—
ideal conditions for a race car.

Highly coveted today:
Rims with the
Rudge central lock

In the mid 1950s, designers in what was called the Stylistics Department in Sindelfingen work on the design of the 300 SL. Different detail variants are conceptualized on a clay model.

(50 kilograms), the new frame was significantly lighter than the 154-pound (70-kilogram) frame from 1939.

In order to maintain stability with this kind of chassis, it is important to keep the cabin very wide where doors would normally be located. This necessity brought about the most spectacular innovation of the 300 SL: the gull-wing doors. When the "Design Center" in Sindelfingen equipped the new frame with the smoothest possible aluminum skin, it was only natural that conventional doors would be omitted. Instead, an entrance hinged at the roof was selected.

This decision was made easier by Alfred Neubauer's knowledge of the rules. After reviewing all the available regulations, he was pleased to find that upward-opening doors were not forbidden anywhere in the rules. Mercedes succeeded in squaring the circle with the 300 SL: The car was full of new solutions that still perfectly adhered to all rule requirements.

For the W 198 II roadster, which
was built from 1957 to 1963,
drafts were first created with
a bold hardtop shape.

If you ask the designers and technicians, years after they succeeded in creating a masterpiece, how exactly this vehicle was able to be created, you will hear again and again how everything came about almost unavoidably—as if the result was actually predestined. In the case of the 300 SL, too, this is of course only a half-truth; it was by no means created accidentally. Rather, it is the result of a process in which every opportunity to gather more information was taken. For instance, technicians also took models into the wind tunnel of the University of Stuttgart, and they made their finishing touches based on the results attained there.

ARCHETYPE OF A BREED
Karl Wilfert and Friedrich Geiger played key roles in visually transforming the race car into the shape we know today. At the time, Geiger was the Head of the Stylistics Department, a pre-

The body was molded from sheet steel, the doors feature rocker panels, the hood, and trunk lid are made of aluminum. For an additional charge, Mercedes built a fully aluminum version that was about 176 pounds (80 kilograms) lighter.

cursor to the present-day design team. Using many dramatic details, he ensured that the 300 SL stood in stark contrast to its more purpose-built contemporaries and became the archetype for a new breed of car. These details include the taillights, a hood with two curved ridges, and the characteristic profile of the car.

A person viewing this sculpture on wheels for the first time is like one bewitched; they are awed, mesmerized by the form, the sound—and the doors that open upward. The 300 SL has hardly lost any of its impact to this day. At auctions, it regularly hits a seven-figure sale price. And then, of course, there was also the

roadster, the design of which Geiger began only a few months after presenting the series-production 300 SL. Explaining how the vehicle, presented at the Geneva Motor Show in 1957, won over experts and customers, Paolo Tumminelli says: "With the dramatic integrated headlights, the invisible cover for the fabric convertible top and, finally, a hardtop that is no mere safety measure, but rather an aesthetic work of art. Whether it is the delicate pagoda roof or a high-tech folding mechanism, its 'hat,' of all things, gives the car its exciting personality: sometimes an exposed sports car for the real feel of fresh air, sometimes a finely dressed coupé for a good journey on any road."

Flawless: On the rear, all elements of the streamlined style fit together perfectly.

The design of the century: The 300 SL was shipped in silver gray as standard.
Other paint colors, such as signal or flame red, were only manufactured on request.

A STAR FOR THE STARS

On the artists, aristocrats, and entrepreneurs who fell for the fascinating 300 SL

For the presentation of the German super-sports car, the Mercedes is parked in front of the French national symbol in the early 1950s. Here, the 300 SL is not called the "Gullwing," but "Papillon"—butterfly.

Car nut Steve McQueen also had a 300 SL of his own. He is pictured here on a joyride
in 1960 with his spouse Neile Adams in Greenwich Village, New York.

There are a variety of factors that help an automobile reach icon status. In addition to the measurable ones, such as the output or successes in motor sports, there are also soft skills, like suitability for TV or film appearances, which further the mythos of a model. At the same time, it can't hurt if a few prominent personages come out as fans of the aspiring automobile legend. This wasn't hard to achieve, thanks to its top performance values. When a Beetle back in the day reached top and continuous speeds of 70 mph (112 km/h), the 300 SL driver would start to think about engaging third gear—and the fourth remaining gear was enough to push it to astronomical speed ranges: up to 162 mph (260 km/h) was possible with the corresponding transmission ratio.

This Gullwing appears to have carried Deep Purple musicians Jon Lord (left) and Tommy Bolin in 1975 above the clouds of Los Angeles.

Actress Sophia Loren has a passion for sports cars. Knowing this, her husband Carlo Ponti gifted her a 300 SL in 1955. The film star and coupé have modeled for countless photo shoots.

In other words, it was a car for real daredevils: drenched with sweat from the driver of a Carrera Panamericana, enveloped by brake dust on the Nürburgring, animated with the aura of a Le Mans winner. No wonder they adored it: King Baudouin of Belgium, King Hussein of Jordan, Prince Ali Khan, Prince Konstantin of Greece, and Argentine President Juan Perón; newspaper magnate William Randolph Hearst Jr., writer John Knittel and—one cannot forget—actor and horsepower-junkie Steve McQueen; as well as conductor Herbert von Karajan, who was smitten with edgy sports cars his whole life. Denizens of heavier music genres also took a shine to the Gullwing. This is how we got the wonderful picture in which John Lord and Tommy Bolin of Deep Purple can be seen with a 300 SL. The soundtrack for this may have been the song "Highway Star," which British magazine *Top Gear* named one of the five "Greatest Driving Songs of All Time": "Nobody gonna take my

The star photographer David Douglas Duncan was a friend of painter Pablo Picasso and his second wife Jacqueline Roque. He produced a photo series in the Swiss Alps in 1956 for *Collier's Magazine* ahead of the market launch of the 300 SL roadster in the US, which became an enormous publicity success for Mercedes.

Yul Brynner in Saint-Tropez, 1960: The actor was among the first buyers of the 300 SL Roadster in the US, along with his colleague Clark Gable.

car, I'm gonna race it to the ground, nobody gonna beat my car, it's gonna break the speed of sound."

The brilliant painter Pablo Picasso was happily photographed and driven around in the black coupé of David D. Duncan. Duncan, one of the most famous photographers of American news magazine *Life*, owned a 300 SL from 1954 on and drove it

for hundred of thousands of miles—including to Moscow in the late 50s. One can imagine how much attention the Gullwing got in front of the Kremlin at the time. By the way, the photographer did not pass way until 2018, at the age of 102 in Grasse, France. Female customers also enjoyed being photographed with the 300 SL: Sophia Loren, Zsa Zsa Gabor, Gina Lollobrigida, and

The Austrian men's team pose in front of a 300 SL at the World Ski Championships in Bad Gastein in 1958: Toni Sailer, Anderl Molterer, coach Toni Spiess, Egon Zimmermann, Hias Leitner, Ernst Hinterseer, Josl Rieder (from right). Sailer won gold three times and silver once.

US actor Ruth Hampton, for instance. For them all, it took some degree of courage to drive the 300 SL—it is an incognito race car, after all.

FROM THE BLITZ FROM KITZ TO THE DICTATOR'S SON

The car became more comfortable starting in 1957, when the Gullwing was replaced by the roadster—after 1400 units built, its refined brother celebrated its premiere. It delighted prominent figures such as ski legend Toni Sailer, the "Blitz from Kitz," and actors Horst Buchholz, Curd Jürgens, Glenn Ford, and Clark Gable. There were also more sinister owners, such as the Dominican dictator's son Rafael L. Trujillo Jr., better known in high society as Ramfis Trujillo, who was known to give a sports car as an offering to women he was enamored with, including Kim Novak and Zsa Zsa Gabor. Allegedly, stickers with ironic statements started turning up on cars on the streets of Los Angeles in the late 1950s: "This car was not a gift from Ramfis Trujillo."

In 1959, actor Horst Buchholz is also a proud 300 SL owner. Approaching the front passenger seat is his wife Miriam Bru Platz. The car bore the chassis number 198.042.7500219.

In 1960, actor Curd Jürgens pilots his Mercedes right up to sound studio 5 on the UFA studio lot in the Tempelhof district of Berlin. It will be parked properly by an employee.

The maharajah of Jaipur added a 300 SL roadster to his collection of Mercedes compressor models, which included a 540 K special roadster—later, a wide range of Mercedes-Benz 600 variants would also join the pack. Austrian actor Gunther Philipp, who was also a successful race car driver in various Ferrari models, also bought himself a 300 SL roadster. Elvis Presley was photographed with a 300 SL when he was stationed in Germany. He also drove a BMW 507 at this time, before he switched to Cadillac.

The 300 SL roadster was more suitable for daily use, easier to enter, possessed a larger trunk, and also had the advantage of having 1850 units built until spring 1963—which is why it is also a little more affordable today. However, the question remains as to whether very high six-figure and low seven-figure amounts can really be called "affordable."

In both variations, the 300 SL contributed significantly to the Daimler-Benz legend. It sold very well, despite its high price tag for the day of 29,000 German marks for the coupé and

Doris Day and Tony Randall (shown) starred in the 1959 Hollywood comedy *Pillow Talk*, next to Rock Hudson and a certain W 198 II. The latter donned a silver-gray metallic exterior and a red leather interior.

32,500 marks for the roadster (plus 1500 marks for the hardtop). The rich, the powerful, and the famous were as passionate then as they are today about owning one of these precious commodities—or at least getting to drive one.

DEFYING THE BOUNDARIES OF GENRE

Another important factor for the ascent up the Mount Olympus of automobile icons is the filmography of a vehicle. This worked perfectly for the Aston Martin DB5 in *Goldfinger*. It is ideal product placement, which means a win for the image of both the film as well as the car (and its manufacturer).

Starting in the late 1950s, the 300 SL developed into a movie hero. It was never limited to any one genre. Its early appearances included the comedies *Pillow Talk* with Doris Day and *Cinderfella* with Jerry Lewis from 1959 and 1960. In its further screen career, it appeared in science-fiction flicks (*The Lost World* from 1960), thrillers (*The Game* from 1997 with Michael Douglas), and action films (*Charlie's Angels* from 2000 with Cameron Diaz, Drew Barrymore, and Bill Murray).

The protagonist of this book had a special part in *Elevator to the Gallows* from 1958. In it, Louis and Veronique race a stolen car against a 300 SL on the freeway. They later meet the German driver of the Mercedes and his wife in a motel. Louis is surprised by the owners during an attempt to steal the car. He kills them and flees with Veronique in the 300 SL.

Classics of the French New Wave: In *Elevator to the Gallows*, Veronique (Yori Bertin) and Louis (Georges Poujouly) are surprised during an attempted theft of a 300 SL. They become embroiled in violence, lies, and deception, all set to a mournful jazz score by Miles Davis.

At the premiere of the film *And Satan Calls the Turns* in 1962, art sponsor Paul-Louis Weiller presents French lead actress Catherine Deneuve in a Gullwing.

A TRUE MASTERPIECE

Elevator to the Gallows, like the 300 SL, is considered a masterpiece, with its dense, dark atmosphere created by director Louis Malle, the fabulous score by Miles Davis, and a performance by Jeanne Moreau that can only be described as raw.

But the Mercedes 300 SL also has a place in the visual arts. In honor of the 100th birthday of the automobile in 1986, Andy Warhol started the commissioned series Cars. The death of the pop-art star in the following year unfortunately prevented the completion of the series. However, in addition to the Silver Arrow, the depiction of the 300 SL is one of the most prominent individual artworks. They are part of the Daimler Art Collection, the corporate group's collection, which now includes more than 1500 objects.

Art meets Gullwing: American artist Kenny Howard, better known as Von Dutch, converted this 300 SL into a visual sea of flames in 1957.

Prince Bertil of Sweden was the Uncle of King Carl XVI Gustaf. He also drove in motor races in the 1930s—under a pseudonym ("Monsieur Adrian") due to his noble status. Here, the "motor prince" tests the Mercedes 300 SL.

Sensation at the New York International Auto Show in 1954: The 300 SL, a racing-turned-series-production vehicle, attracts attention in the professional world both visually as well as technologically, thanks to its gasoline direct injection.

Visual trickery: Photographer René Staud leaves the car on the ground but, by draping all
other objects so skillfully, the convertible appears to hang on the wall like a painting.

Für die Wohlfahrtspflege
Deutschland

300 SL

+55
25

Baujahr 1954   Länge 4520 mm   Breite 1790 mm   Höhe 1300 mm

Immortalized as a postage stamp: In 2002, the German welfare association releases a postage stamp with the motif of the 300 SL, designed by Lorli and Ernst Jünger.

The Mercedes Gullwing was elevated to a special kind of art object by Von Dutch. Born in 1929, Von Dutch (real name: Kenneth Robert Howard) was a thoroughly contradictory figure: while he had highly questionable ethics politically—contemporaries described him as racist—he was also a pioneer of the Kustom Kulture movement. For his friend, bar owner Earl Bruce, he emblazoned a Gullwing with a pattern of flickering flames.

The Mercedes 300 SL also has a spot as a true masterpiece in exhibitions and museums. It was a must-have in the large sports-car design exhibition "PS: Ich liebe Dich. Sportwagen-Design der 1950er bis 1970er Jahre," which took place in the Museum Kunstpalast in Dusseldorf in 2018/2019. A little further south along the Rhine, the 300 SL is a permanent fixture in the design wing of the Museum of Applied Art Cologne (MAKK).

The "master of light," René Staud, has long had a weakness for the Gullwing. For decades, the photographer has payed homage to the fascinating SL in various publications, calendars, and books. A car like this, with shapes as clear as they are dramatic, is ideally suited for Staud's art. He understands better than anyone else how to accentuate the lines of a vehicle with his lighting.

Another indicator of whether an automobile has made its way into the collective memory is its use as a stamp design. From 2002 to 2008, the German Federal Association of Non-statutory Welfare released four series on the subject of means of transportation. The Gullwing is featured in the "Oldtimer I" series, next to the bubble car (BMW Isetta 300), Beetle (VW Type 1), Trabbi (Sachsenring Trabant P50), and "Leukoplastbomber" (Borgward Isabella Coupé). Viewed in this context, one might also say that a nickname is almost mandatory for car legend status.

LEGEND-FORMING LEGENDS

Speaking of legends: Even on dry land, vehicle enthusiasts like to spin yarns, too. There are many such tall tales concerning the creation of the 300 SL that reside in the gray zone between truth and fiction.

One of the most widespread concerns Max Hoffman, the Mercedes-Benz importer for the US and Canada. He is said not only to have pushed the factory to develop a road version from

A 300 SL parade at the 38th annual meeting of the Gull Wing Group International on September 16, 2006 at the Hyatt Regency Lake Tahoe Resort in Incline Village, Nevada, USA

The dream of all fans of the classic automobile:
A picture of the annual meeting for the 40th anniversary
of the German Mercedes-Benz 300 SL Club,
held from June 21 to 24, 2018 in Fulda.

the race car and also produce a smaller sports car at the same time—the 190 SL—for the enormous US market; it is also said that he baited the company by backing up his desire with an order of 1000 units of the 300 SL.

Regardless of the fact that an order of this type has never been found in the archive, Heinz Hoppe, a representative for Daimler-Benz in the US starting in 1954, then Head of Daimler-Benz of North America for years and later a sales executive in Stuttgart, doesn't remember any such offer either. "Maxie Hoffman was a brilliant salesman with a definite intui-

tion about what could be sold. This is how he brought Porsche, Jaguar, and Ferrari, among others, to the US; but his biggest coup was a contract with BMW, which secured him the distribution rights for the Bavarian brand (with an unlimited duration)—a contract that cost BMW a lot of money when it wanted to set up its own sales organization. However, Hoffman was intelligent enough not to sign any contract for 1000 unsold cars. What is true is that Hoffman understood the market and constantly pushed for the car to be built because he knew his rich clientèle."

In Japan, passengers have to pay the toll—right-hand drive vehicles were never built. The photograph comes from the Gumball 3000, one of the most exciting automotive events of our times. The 2018 tour took participants from London to Tokyo.

Whether or not they are true, such stories and anecdotes also help a vehicle become a legend.

COME TOGETHER

It seems that many individual components do their part to turn a simple automobile into a cult object. The most important component of all, however, is the people who develop a special passion for a brand or model. This passion spreads out into the fan clubs where enthusiasts congregate. In Germany, the Mercedes-Benz 300 SL Club honors the legacy of the vehicle. Its goals include the maintenance and preservation of existing models, of which there were about 500 in Germany in 2019. The annual meeting of the group has been held since 1978. There, members from Germany and abroad meet, rare vehicles are exhibited, and fan culture is nurtured.

The transatlantic counterpart is even older. The Gull Wing Group International was founded in 1961 in San Francisco by 18 SL enthusiasts. At the first annual meeting in 1969, around

Test drives in California: The Willow Springs Raceway in Rosamond is a curving course, highly demanding on both drivers and automobiles. Mercedes tested the 300 SL here in 1956.

100 members traveled to Reno, Nevada. Meetings still take place annually today, although there are now about 600 members from 22 countries.

VIP GUEST

The Mercedes 300 SL is also a welcomed guest at other events, such as at the large Concours d'Élégance in Pebble Beach, California, and at the Grand Hotel Villa d'Este on Lake Como. It regularly wins beauty contests there. Recently, a 300 SL at the 2019 concours on Lake Como was the winner in class C, "A new dawn: Into the rock'n'roll era."

A 300 SL can be seen from time to time in classic car racing events, be they in Goodwood or at the modern incarnation of the Mille Miglia. It grabs as much attention there as it does at the Gumball 3000. A Gullwing took part in its twentieth event—a mix of motor rally, concours, and lifestyle event, or, in the words of its founder Maximillion Cooper, a "rolling rock'n'roll party"—on the tour from London to Tokyo in 2018.

Lake Bonneville, a dry salt lake in Utah, USA, is ideal for high-speed driving. In 1956, the Gullwing of Albert L. Schmidt delivered an average speed of 148.131 mph (238.393 km/h).

With the start number 417, John Fitch and Kurt Gesell took the class win and placed 5th in the overall ranking at the Mille Miglia in 1955—and in 2017, on the occasion of the 75th Member's Meeting, the classic car started in the legendary race on the Goodwood Circuit in the South of England.

Next to the Targa Florio, the Mille Miglia was considered the most difficult endurance race for sports cars up to the end of 1957.
Since 1977, a tour with historic vehicles has been organized under this name—and a 300 SL is guaranteed to be present each year.

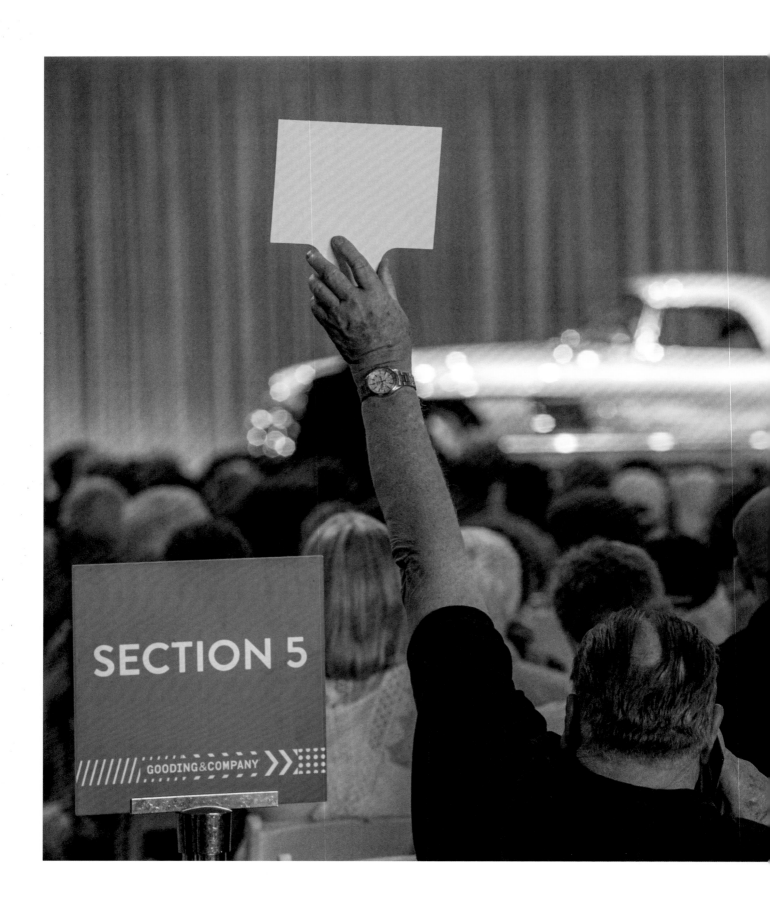

The Pebble Beach Concours d'Elegance is an annual beauty contest for historic automobiles in Monterey, California. On the sidelines of the event, classic cars such as this 300 SL from 1955 are also auctioned off. In 2017, this car went to the highest bidder for 1,677,500 US dollars. The estimated value was previously between one and 1.3 million US dollars.

In its history, the Gullwing has also driven on some unusual terrain. At the eighth Bonneville National Speed Trials on the Bonneville Salt Flats in Utah, Albert L. Schmidt reached an average speed of just under 149 mph (240 km/h) in the 300 SL. Clearly, the Mercedes 300 SL has an impressive logbook. It has taken part in the most important events, celebrated wins in motor sports, passed its screen test, and stood in the garages of many celebrities. What's more, it makes an impression with its dramatic exterior, and the number of units still available is quite manageable. Its reputation as the "sports car of the century" is excellent. Of course, this also makes it a coveted collector's item.

When it goes up at large auction houses like Sotheby's, Artcurial, or Bonhams, the 300 SL rakes in top dollar. Depending on the condition and origin, seven-figure prices are not unusual. In 2018, a spectacular garage find brought in 1.3 million euros for the auction house Gooding. The provenance of the car was also extraordinary: at one point, the car had belonged to Herbert von Karajan.

Elegant
beherrschte
Kraft

ROADSTER

Wo man sich für die gebändigte Kraft eines starken Motors begeistert, wo man ein erregendes Fahrerlebnis in einem faszinierenden Wagen sucht, da steht der neue Mercedes-Benz 300 SL Roadster im Mittelpunkt des Interesses. Leicht und elegant beherrschen Sie die geschmeidige Kraft dieses modernen Seriensportwagens, denn seine 225 PS liegen sicher in Ihrer Hand. Form, Leistung und Fahreigenschaften reiften in diesem dynamischen Wagen zu vollendeter Harmonie.

MERCEDES-BENZ Ihr guter Stern auf allen Straßen

While gasoline producers put a tiger in the tank,
Mercedes-Benz let him run free.

Strength, performance, victories: From the beginning, the corporate communication made no secret of the advantages of the 300 SL. The illustrations on this and the following page come from Austrian painter, commercial artist, and illustrator Hans Liska, who created the models for the Mercedes-Benz brochures for decades.

Leistung voraus TYP 300 SL

Den Gewinn aller Siege des Mercedes-Sterns legen die Konstrukteure der Daimler-Benz AG. mit diesem Sportwagen von souveräner Eleganz in die Hände ihrer Kunden.

190 SL

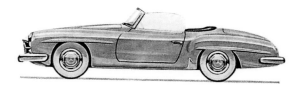

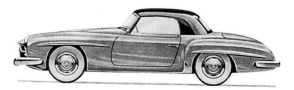

in jeder Form vollendet

Ob als Roadster oder mit Coupé-Dach gefahren -

was die vollendete Form seiner Karosserie an dynamischem Schwung erkennen läßt,

wird für Sie am Steuer des 190 SL zu einem begeisternden Erlebnis.

IHR GUTER STERN AUF ALLEN STRASSEN  **MERCEDES-BENZ**

For the somewhat less powerful 190 SL, built from 1955 to 1963, other advantages were emphasized: design, versatility—it was basically a perfect recreational vehicle with enough power under the hood.

Reaching for the stars: For a contemporary promotional photo in 1960, a 300 SL posed next to a North American F-86D Sabre, the Sabre Dog, a U.S. Air Force interceptor plane.

This freshly coiffed young woman must wear gloves to approach the new W 198 II: In 1957, the young country of West Germany is already registering full employm and the 300 SL roadster serves as a symbol of the new wealth. Mercedes produced exactly 1858 units up to 1963. The price started at 32,500 German marks.

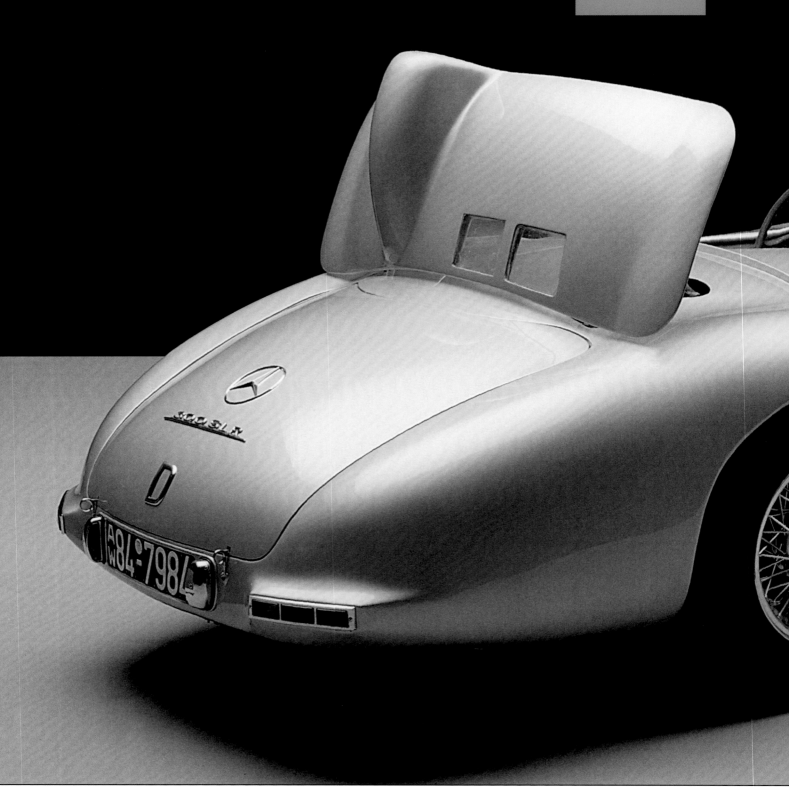

There was a "Le Mans version" of the thoroughbred 300 SLR race car (W 196 S) which featured "air brakes": using a lever, the driver could position a flap in the airstream hydraulically in order to boost the power of the drum brakes.

A PERFECT BLEND FOR THE SENSES

The eventful development history of a legend on racetrack and road

300 SL RACE CAR (W 194)

Production years: 1952–1953

Engine: In-line six-cylinder engine with carburetor

Displacement: 2996 cm^3

Output: 129 kW (175 metric HP) at 5200 rpm

Acceleration 0-62 mph (0–100 km/h): 7.5 s

Top speed: 149 mph (240 km/h)

Weight: 1916 lbs. (869 kg)

Dimensions (L x W x H): 166 x 70 x 50 in (4220 x 1790 x 1265 mm)

Quantity: 10

300 SL PROTOTYPE (W 194)

Production years: 1953

Engine: In-line six-cylinder engine with direct injection

Displacement: 2996 cm³

Output: 167 kW (225 metric HP) at 6000 rpm

Acceleration 0-62 mph (0–100 km/h): 7 s

Top speed: 162 mph (260 km/h)

Weight: 2094 lbs. (950 kg)

Dimensions (L x W x H): 161 x 70 x 50 in (4100 x 1790 x 1265 mm)

Quantity: 1

Because the genesis of the Mercedes-Benz 300 SL is intimately connected to motor sports, one could use the metaphor of a "flying start" to describe the initial situation. For the series' archetype, the 300 SL racecar, it was necessary to make do with the elements on hand in light of the constraints posed by the situation in postwar Germany and the available resources. Rather than starting from scratch, the engineers used the 300 series sedan as a building block of sorts, which proved to be both a curse and a blessing. The M 186 engine's weight and output did not exactly inspire enthusiasm on the part of Alfred Neubauer, the racing manager. For want of alternatives, however, "Don Alfredo" got on board with the approach.

Certain parts, such as the front and rear axles, required only slight modification. More substantial changes were made to the engine because the technicians soon realized that they had to more or less match the over 200 horsepower that competitors Ferrari, Jaguar, Talbot, and Cunningham were achieving. When working on the six-cylinder, however, Mercedes quickly became aware that this goal was unattainable—thus the aim was lowered slightly to 180 horsepower. Improved dynamics were intended to compensate for the lack of horsepower.

A number of design coups, including the engine's 50-degree incline, the grill pipe framework, and the gull-wing doors ensured that the target specifications were met. This made the 300 SL not just competitive in motor racing, but a real champion.

Rudolf Uhlenhaut, Head of the Racecar Department, qualified this somewhat. "The '52 races showed that the 300 SL with naturally aspirated engine was—in terms of the final speed—at least on a par with even the strongest competitors, if not even superior. In acceleration on good roads, however, it clearly lagged behind the Ferrari 4.1 liter, while also lagging somewhat behind the Ferrari 3 liter and the Gordini 2.3 liter. However, the competitors' lack of operating safety and reliability and the stamina of the 300 SL generally meant a win for our brand."

THE "PLANE" BUILDS BRIDGES

Correspondingly, further development work started in 1952. Despite an executive board resolution to the contrary, plans originally called for participation in sports car races in 1953. However, this plan was forsaken in order to concentrate fully on the 1954 season of the Grand Prix, the predecessor to Formula One.

Therefore, the company manufactured just one of the "planes," as the vehicle was nicknamed internally because the shape of its front section resembled this tool. However, this one-off had immense significance. It was a bridge between the 1952 race car and the series production vehicle presented in 1954. In terms of technology and aerodynamics, Rudolf Uhlenhaut and his team had clearly surpassed the race car. A changeover from the carburetor engine to gasoline direct injection resulted in a significant increase in performance.

When the 300 SL Coupé was presented in New York in 1954, the series model had adopted some features from the 1953 prototype, including the injection technology of the six-cylinder engine. With a great deal of fine tuning, the engine was trimmed down to 215 horsepower— however, this output was reached only

300 SL COUPÉ (W 198 I)

Production years: 1954–1957

Engine: In-line six-cylinder engine with direct injection

Displacement: 2996 cm³

Output: 158 kW (215 metric HP) at 5800 rpm

Acceleration 0-62 mph (0–100 km/h): 10 s

Top speed: 162 mph (260 km/h)

Weight: 2855 lbs. (1295 kg)

Dimensions (L x W x H): 178 x 70 x 51 in (4520 x 1790 x 1300 mm)

Quantity: 1400

The 300 SLR with start number 722, driven by Stirling Moss and Denis Jenkinson, won the Mille Miglia in 1955 with a record time that was never beaten and an average speed of 97.959 mph (157.650 km/h). Nine chassis were created—of those, two are coupés.

300 SLR (W 196 S)

Production years: 1955
Engine: Eight-cylinder in-line engine with
    direct injection
Displacement: 2982 cm³
Output: 228 kW (310 metric HP) at 7400 rpm
Acceleration 0-62 mph (0–100 km/h): 6.8 s
Top speed: over 186 mph (300 km/h)
Weight: 1984 lbs. (900 kg)
Dimensions (L x W x H): 169 x 69 x 43 in
    (4300 x 1740 x 1100 mm)
Quantity: 9 chassis (of those, 2 coupés)

300 SLR
"UHLENHAUT COUPÉ"

Production years: 1955
Engine: Eight-cylinder in-line engine with
    direct injection
Displacement: 2982 cm³
Output: 228 kW (310 metric HP) at 7400 rpm
Acceleration 0-62 mph (0–100 km/h): 6.8 s
Top speed: 176 mph (284 km/h)
Weight: 2463 lbs. (1117 kg)
Dimensions (L x W x H): 171 x 69 x 48 in
    (4350 x 1750 x 1210 mm)
Quantity: 2

with the sports camshaft available as special equipment. The series version of the in-line six-cylinder engine was equipped with the camshaft of the first 300 from 1951, which provided 200 horsepower. However, because most coupés were equipped with the sports camshaft—which was installed as series equipment in the 300 SL Roadster—the output of 215 horsepower has now become established in the public's mind as a baseline.

MISSION ACCOMPLISHED

All in all, the Daimler-Benz technicians fulfilled their assignment very well, despite minor weaknesses. The race car had become a GT car suitable for daily use that combined the driving performance of the 1952 race cars with passable comfort and convenience and an acceptable trunk size. However, the car had also gained a significant amount of weight compared to the race car—the in-line six-cylinder engine now had over 400 more pounds (200 kilograms) to transport.

In summary, the 300 SL was an interesting blend: A car that, in its original form, could be used in the 1952 races only because management was able to convince Alfred Neubauer to accept it in spite of its weaknesses. A car with too little output that Neubauer would have never let cross the starting line had he had a choice—but which seamlessly continued the legend of the "Silver Arrows" all the same. Originally, it was to be entered in the race in 1953—Rudolf Uhlenhaut had given it all the refinements for this purpose. But it would not appear at the races that year—the engineers would ultimately use the knowledge for the series-production car of 1954. The management's decision to produce it at all was owed to the persuasive power of Max Hoffman. The US importer had convinced the board in Untertürkheim with his instinct for the desires of American buyers.

In 1953, Mercedes-Benz decided to return to Grand Prix races with its best engineers and significant financial com-

mitment, which would result in winning world championship titles in 1954 and 1955. At the same time, the engineers discovered that the 2.5-liter in-line eight-cylinder engine could also be used in the races for the World Sportscar Championship by enlarging the displacement to three liters. This lead to the development of the 300 SLR sports car, which seized its second world championship in 1955—concurrent to the second win of the Formula 1 title. The Uhlenhaut Coupé even more famous, however. Only two units were ever built of the 300 SLR coupé, which featured a racing engine and a top speed over 174 mph (280 km/h), and which the head engineer drove in daily traffic.

WORTHY SUCCESSOR:
THE ROADSTER

The 300 SL roadster was presented at the Geneva Motor Show in March 1957. As with the coupé, importer Max Hoffman also provided key motivation for the development of the roadster. He had known that there was desire for a degree of comfort, especially on the American

300 SL ROADSTER (W 198 II)

Production years: 1957–1963

Engine: In-line six-cylinder engine with
   direct injection

Displacement: 2996 cm³

Output: 158 kW (215 metric HP) at 5800 rpm

Acceleration 0-62 mph (0–100 km/h): 10 s

Top speed: 155 mph (250 km/h)

Weight: 3131 lbs. (1420 kg)

Dimensions (L x W x H): 180 x 70 x 51 in
   (4570 x 1790 x 1300 mm)

Quantity: 1858

market, which the coupé lacked. Production of the roadster began in 1957, and that of the coupé was discontinued in the same year.

Of course, a tubular frame also provided the necessary torsional strength in the roadster, but it now had "normal" doors and the single-joint swing axle, which had been featured on the prototype from 1953, in order to improve driving dynamics. With a top speed of 155 mph (250 km/h), the 300 SL roadster was also among the fastest vehicles on the roads, doing justice to its heritage as the successor of the race car from 1952.

ADVANCEMENT THROUGH IDEAS

The 300 SL proves that necessity can provide fertile ground for innovations

The chassis exposed: The vehicle frame of the W 198 roadster needed to be bend-resistant and torsionally rigid in order to absorb acceleration and braking forces.

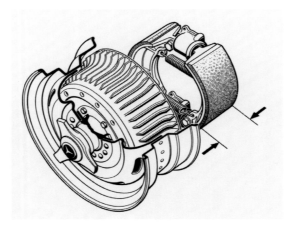

The Mercedes-Benz 300 SL performed as well on the racetrack as it did with rich clients as a series-production vehicle, but that was not the end of its hybrid nature. It also represented a perfect symbiosis of elegance and sportiness, ease, and power.

As John Bolster wrote in *Autosport*, "The Mercedes-Benz 300 SL is a car of beautiful appearance and almost incredible performance. Its construction and finish are of the very highest class, and its whole design represents a technical tour de force."

When talking about these new ideas, the tubular space frame and gull-wing doors usually come to mind first. But there were also concepts that did not win a spot in automobile history. These include the "air brake," used for improved road-holding during the training for the 24-hour race in Le Mans in 1952.

Sectional view of a drum brake. The brakes for the series production vehicle were adopted directly from the race car from 1952—however, for production technology reasons, somewhat coarser ribbing was used.

This extra wing on the Gullwing did not stand the test, despite how visually striking it is *(see page 104)*.

THE FIRST FORMULA FOR SUCCESS:
TUBULAR SPACE FRAME + GULL-WING DOORS

While the multisyllabic phrase does not exactly roll off the tongue, the innovation of the tubular space frame nonetheless plays an important role in the development of the 300 SL.

Since options for optimizing the engine of its predecessor, the Mercedes-Benz 300, for the 300 SL were limited, engineers had to make other adjustments during development. Possible improvements were found primarily in the areas of aerodynamics and weight.

The vehicle was to be a light-weight construction. The vehicle frame needed to be bend-resistant and torsionally rigid in order to absorb the acceleration and braking forces. The most advan-

Highly praised: the tubular frame gives the sports car tremendous stability despite its low weight

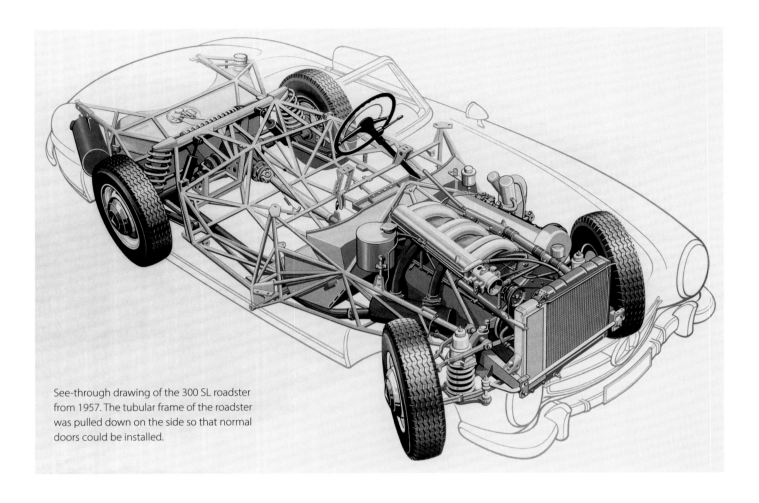

See-through drawing of the 300 SL roadster from 1957. The tubular frame of the roadster was pulled down on the side so that normal doors could be installed.

tageous design was a tubular frame, in which tubes have to absorb the tensile and compressive forces. With consideration for the ease of entry of the low coupé model, which had proved especially favorable in wind tunnel measurements, doors that open upwards were developed. As a result, a very high side frame section was able to be designed, simultaneously increasing the bending resistance of the entire frame. The result—a finished tubular frame with mounting plates and supports for the engine, power units, and axles—weighed just 181 pounds (82 kilograms) and was later adopted for the series-production 300 SL sports car.

Rudolf Uhlenhaut was largely to thank for the trick with the tubular frame, which had a low weight (important in the absence of power) while still offering enormous stability (important for the driving characteristics and the curve speeds to be achieved). A comparison with the tubular ladder frame of the pre-war W 154 race car provided a reference point for the excellent rigidity of this tubular space frame. Both frames

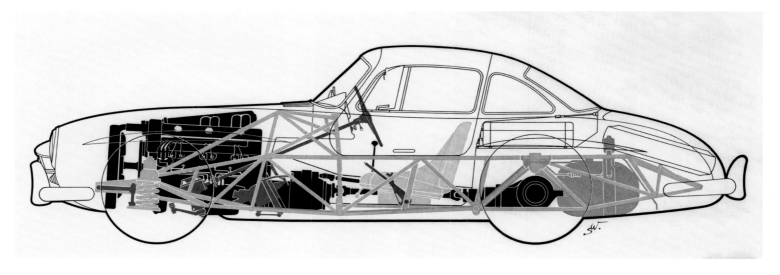

300 SL coupé from 1954 in profile: Note how the trunk is mostly filled by a spare wheel and 26.4-gallon (100-liter) tank.

The 300 SL was exclusively produced with left-hand drive: Due to the severe inclination of the engine and the intake ducts and exhaust pipes running down the right side, a right-hand drive system was impossible to install.

feature the same resistance to warping, but the new one weighed just 110 pounds (50 kilograms), compared to the 154-pound (70-kilogram) frame from 1939.

THE SECOND FORMULA FOR SUCCESS:
ENGINE INCLINATION + DIRECT INJECTION

Some interesting ideas were also implemented under the hood of the 300 SL. The engine of the 300 SL was closely based on the M 186 of the predecessor model. However, it still packed in

a few technical marvels. In order to ensure the required aero-dynamics, the in-line six-cylinder engine was tilted 50 degrees to the left. The increased legroom for the driver due to this arrangement was a pleasant bonus; the fact that this space had been taken from the passenger side had to be tolerated.

In this context, it is notable that all coupés and roadsters were delivered with left-hand drive. Due to the severe inclination of the engine and the intake ducts and exhaust pipes running down the right side, a right-hand drive system could not be

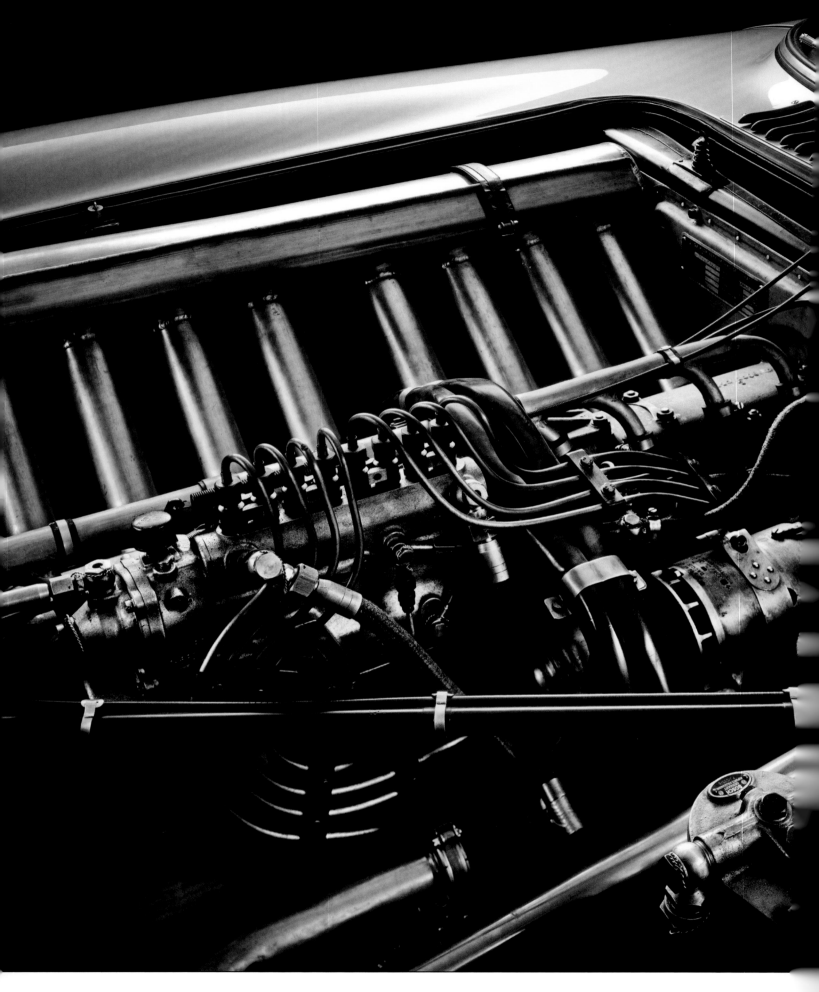

The engine of the "Uhlenhaut Coupé" from 1955: It outputs 302 metric HP and has a top speed of 180 mph (290 km/h)—making it the fastest road-legal car at the time.

installed. However, there is also a famous exception to this: an Australian owner was able to convert his 300 SL into a right-hand drive vehicle—with significant technical effort and financial expense.

Many elements from the 1953 prototype were adopted in the series production model of the 300 SL, including the injection engine. As a result, it was the first series production car with a four-stroke engine to use this technology. Dipl.-Ing. (Graduate Engineer) K. Müller from the Engineering Department of Daimler-Benz wrote about the engine of the 300 SL in May 1957: "While the 300 SL used in the sports car races of 1952 was equipped with the carburetor engine, the first bench tests with gasoline injection in the cylinders had already begun during the

racing season. This enhanced engine provided good data for the development of the 2.5-liter formula race car that was now planned, as well as such a good performance increase with substantial fuel savings that this injection engine was chosen for the series production of the 300 SL. Gasoline injection also provided an excellent transition from idling to maximum speeds of approximately 6000 revolutions per minute. With the high-compression engine and with the high overall ratio in direct gear, this fact makes it possible to drive in city traffic at 25 mph (40 km/h), rev up the engine without stuttering and accelerate up to 143 or 162 mph (230 or 260 km/h)—depending on the rear axle ratio."

The first series production four-stroke engine with direct injection in a passenger car is the six-cylinder M 198 from 1954. It is tilted to the left in the 300 SL.

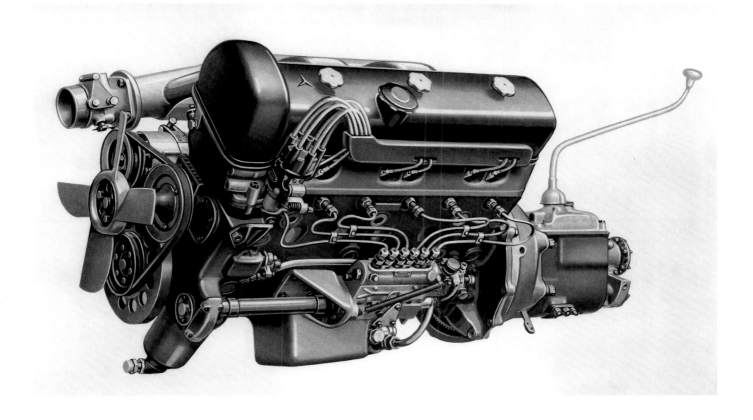

Le Mans 1952: During training for the 24-hour race, Mercedes debuts an aerodynamic aid. The idea of the "air brake" came from racing manager Alfred Neubauer. The impact on the morale of the competition is greater than its actual effect: due to problems with the pylons, this technology is not used in the race.

Some collectors have had the four-spoke steering wheel
of the race cars installed in their vehicles.

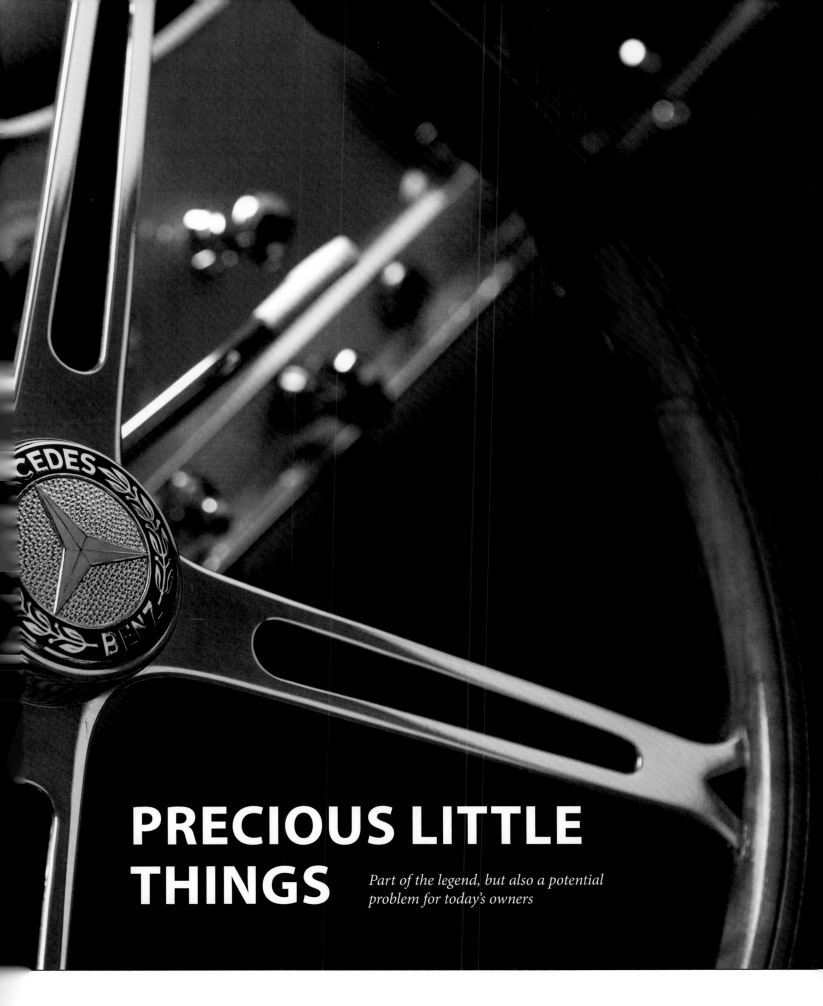

PRECIOUS LITTLE THINGS

Part of the legend, but also a potential problem for today's owners

The expression "attention to detail" describes more than just being a stickler; it entails a process of respect for the little things when working on a whole. The Mercedes-Benz 300 SL is a remarkable example of what attention to detail can do.

A DREAM OF CHROME AND LEATHER

Of course, the 300 SL is primarily prized for its design vocabulary and performance. But there are also little things that continue to excite to this day. The ski rack is a rather fun curiosity, shown on the opposite page. Details like the bumper guards, the dramatic rear lights, or that characteristic decoration on the sides of the car—the air intake!—leave those who see them today almost in awe.

And then there is the interior: In the 300 SL coupé, there were finely upholstered seats, a complete dashboard with a large speedometer, and a tachometer. To the left and right of the steering wheel, which could be removed with a quick-release fastener for an easier entrance and exit, there were two smaller round instruments on each side which provided information about the water

Taking a sports car on winter vacation? Mercedes makes it possible thanks to a ski rack on the 300 SL.

temperature, fuel pressure, oil temperature, and pressure. There was no fuel gauge; in its place, a stopwatch was installed in the center of the dashboard. The 300 SL was still a sports car, after all, even if a refined one. As a whole, the interior of the 300 SL is a dream of chrome and leather.

THE SPARE-PARTS SITUATION

And today? The issue of details still provides another dimension for collectors and owners. Klaus Kienle, an expert in the field of 300 SLs, provides an example of the difficulties one might encounter when trying to keep a 300 SL in original condition: "There are no longer any original housings and seals for the R3 and R8 pumps. Bosch brought out a new housing for the R8 pump, though, and the inner seal of the pump is also significantly improved. This new pump is available as an exchange, provided that you can supply an exchangeable old R8 pump. There is no replacement option for the delivery of a R3 pump—the only option here is the new purchase of an R8 pump. The brake cylinders for the disk brake system are available again, meaning problems can be solved quickly. Instruments for the

A photo like those from *Architectural Digest*: The chrome-and-leather interior with rearview mirror, on-board clock, ventilation, etc.—and yes, an ashtray with integrated cigarette lighter. A snapshot from a time when smoking was still fun.

vehicles are still out of stock. However, thanks to a good inventory of spare parts, restorers have access to them so almost every instrument can be kept in excellent condition. And body components no longer pose a problem for the two types anymore, either—everything is available here. The same is true for reproductions of the window glass and their rubber edges."

So how is a 300 SL perfectly restored? "The improved spare parts situation naturally makes restoration processes easier. Nonetheless, you still need to keep your eyes peeled for original parts, which come on the market now and then. You still need manual labor, plain and simple, to produce or machine special spare parts in single-item production. In short, you could say that restoration for the most part has gotten easier than it was, but the cost of labor and parts has only increased."

It is no wonder that a full restoration can easily take one to two years and cost somewhere in the six-figure range. But who dwells on money when the result is such an artful automobile with all its splendid details?

Whether the bumpers actually
protect the valuable body from
damage is up for debate.

If you ordered a hardtop for your 300 SL roadster back in the day, you made a good choice—today, an original hardtop costs a fortune.

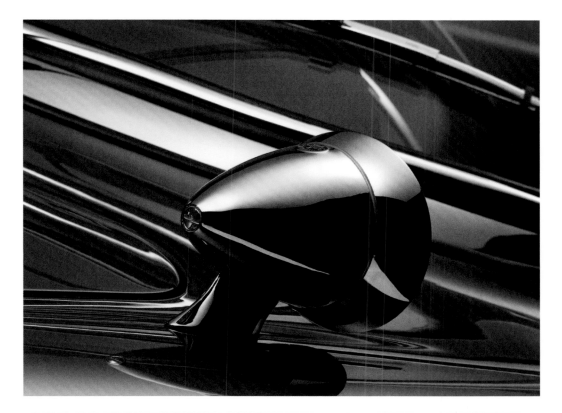

Rearview mirrors from Talbot were considered extra aerodynamic and sporty in the 1950s and 60s—they were used by many manufacturers.

Rims with a central lock were in demand in motor sports—it allowed them to be changed more quickly. They were also ordered on series production models.

The start at the 24 Hours of Le Mans in 1952: In the foreground, the two later winners with the 300 SL (W 194). Second place is taken by Theo Helfrich and Helmut Niedermayr with start number 20. The winners are Hermann Lang and Fritz Riess in number 21.

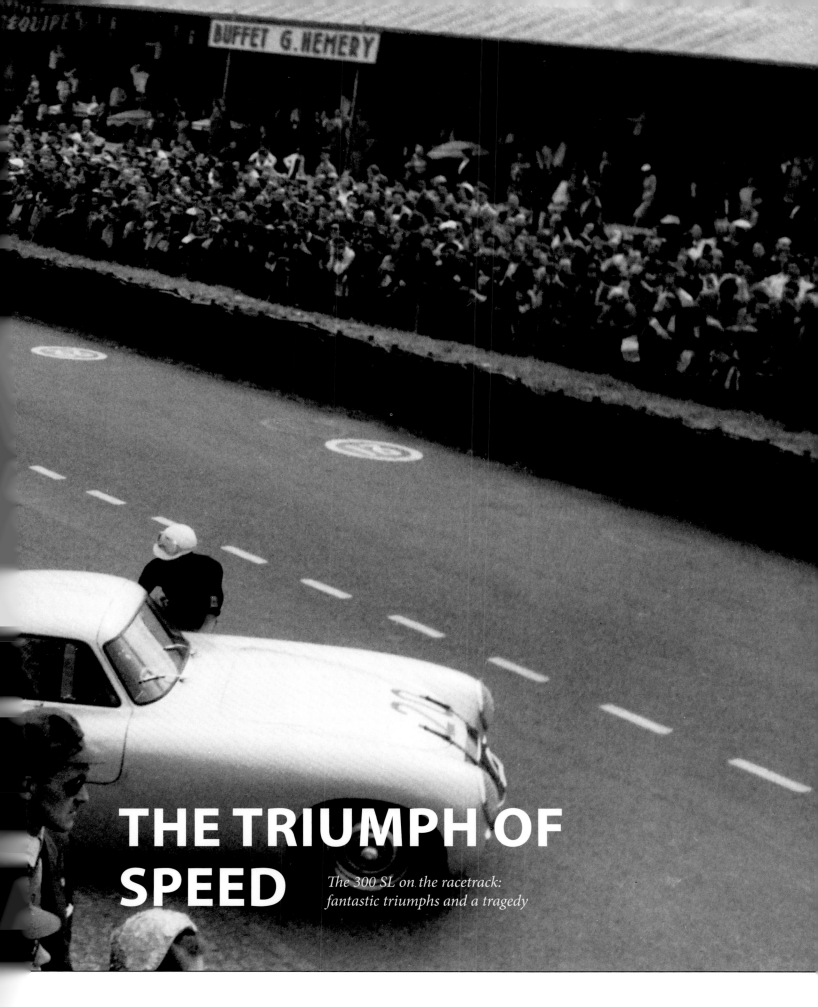

THE TRIUMPH OF
SPEED

The 300 SL on the racetrack:
fantastic triumphs and a tragedy

The maxim "live fast, die young" is generally associated with pop culture figures like James Dean or Janis Joplin. The 300 SL had the four-wheeled equivalent: while it had a short career, it was always in the fast lane.

Less than a year passed between the board's decision to build a sports car until the first race. Another six months transpired from its first use in racing until the presentation of the series production vehicle. The build period of the 300 SL coupé was three years. The racing career of the original 300 SL was a little over half a year. But this period of just under seven months in 1952 had a tremendous impact. This is where a considerable portion of the mythos surrounding the 300 SL originated: four victories in five races

under exciting conditions. The racing history of the 300 SL, then incarnated as the 300 SLR, had a tragic end, however—in one of the biggest motor sports catastrophes in Le Mans in 1955.

MILLE MIGLIA: SLOWED DOWN BY A NUT

Next to the 24 Hours of Le Mans, the Mille Miglia was the ultimate racing event in the 1950s. Armed with a picnic basket and a bottle of Lambrusco, millions of Italians made the pilgrimage to the 994-mile (1600-kilometer) racetrack which once stretched across the country. School was out on this day, of course—and in the factories and office buildings, too, only middling enthusiasm could be mustered during the race.

The race, founded in 1927, was a bastion for Alfa Romeo and Ferrari—Daimler-Benz was only able to win once: In 1931, Rudolf Caracciola was the first non-Italian to drive a legendary Mercedes SSK to victory. And so the brand-new 300 SL made its first journey to Brescia, the starting point of the race.

The race itself took place on May 3 and 4. Daimler-Benz brought three cars to the starting line. These had vehicle identification numbers 00003/52, 00004/52, and 00005/52. Number 3 was driven by Hermann Lang and his co-driver Erwin Grupp with the start number 626, then came Karl Kling and Hans Klenk in number 4 (start number 623). Then, 21 years after his win in a SSK, Rudolf Caracciola appeared with co-driver Peter Kurrle in

The fifth 300 SL built appeared at the Mille Miglia with Rudolf Caracciola behind the wheel. He drove the car without a co-driver to fourth place in the overall ranking.

Preparations for the start of the
Berne Grand Prix, held on May 18,
1952 on the Bremgarten track:
Mercedes entered four cars;
the 300 SL of Hermann Lang
bore the number 20.

the car with vehicle identification number 5 and start number 613.

Karl Kling and Ferrari driver Giovanni Bracco chased each other over the 1000 miles. While Kling was still in the lead at the halfway point in Rome, he ultimately had to admit defeat to the ferocious driving of the Italian in Brescia by a difference of 4:32 minutes. Would Kling have won if a stuck central lock nut during a tire change hadn't cost him six minutes? Still, after 12:14.17 hours of driving at an average speed of 79.4 mph (127.8 km/h), second place in the overall ranking was a sensational start.

Caracciola and Kurrle took 12:40.05 hours in their somewhat weaker car and came in fourth, while Hermann Lang had to give up after just a few miles after grazing a curb with a rear wheel and bending the rear axle in the process.

GRAND PRIX IN BERNE: DOUBLE VICTORY AND A CAREER END

In 1952, the Swiss Grand Prix was the high point of the Alpine country's racing calendar. To ensure an exciting supporting program for the Formula 1 precursor event, the organizers advertised two sports car races: the Bremgarten race for cars with a displacement up to 1.5 liters and the Berne race for race cars with a displacement above 1.5 liters.

Start of the "Prix de Bern": In the first row, the two Mercedes of Rudolf Caracciola (start number 16) and Karl Kling (18) as well as the fastest during training, Willy Peter Daetwyler in Ferrari 340 America (26). Hermann Lang is behind them. For easier differentiation, the 300 SLs were painted differently.

Since Mercedes was not equipped for the 2-liter GP class introduced in 1952, racing manager Alfred Neubauer took the opportunity to showcase the 300 SL in sports car racing—after all, Switzerland was an important market.

Therefore, on May 18 at 1:50 p.m., the 300 SL made its way to the starting line for the second time. Four vehicles had appeared for training the day prior: The car with vehicle identification number

00003/52 was driven by Hermann Lang; the coupé, painted light blue for this race, would take second place in the overall ranking. Karl Kling drove the 00004/52 again; the car with license number W 59-4997, painted green this time, had also been entrusted to him in the Mille Miglia. Number 00005/52 was again driven by Rudolf Caracciola, though it now bore the start number 16 and an eggplant-colored finish. Fritz

Riess had been given the car with number 00002/52, the second version of the first 300 SL series, the only one in the customary silver.

The training times promised an interesting fight: Swiss Willy Peter Daetwyler, in his 4.1-liter Ferrari, was clearly the fastest at 2:55.6 minutes. That corresponded to an average speed of 92.738 mph (149.248 km/h). But it was then followed by the four 300 SLs: Karl Kling

Triple victory for Mercedes-Benz. Karl Kling flies over the finish line, ahead of Hermann Lang and Fritz Riess, who started last.

Daetwyler has to give up in the first lap thanks to a broken drive shaft; Caracciola (16) takes the lead ahead of Kling (18).

with 3:00.1 minutes, Hermann Lang with 3:03.3, Rudolf Caracciola with 3:04.1, and Fritz Riess with 3:07.7. When the fastest car in the training race dropped out just 164 feet (50 meters) after the start due to a broken drive shaft, Caracciola immediately took the lead; he was then overtaken by Lang one lap later. Kling also passed them in the fifth lap, and Riess, who started from the last position, had worked his way up to fourth place.

Karl Kling won ahead of Hermann Lang—who, despite a record lap of 2:56.1 minutes, could not pass him—and Fritz Riess, who was already a whole lap behind. Two Aston Martins and two Lancia Aurelias came next, but Caracciola had had an accident: "It was in the 13th lap. Going 118 mph (190 km/h), I rushed toward the Forsthaus curve and prepared to shift down a gear. When I lightly tapped the brakes, the jaws on the

right side of the car suddenly jammed, and I was pushed to the edge of the slope. At the speed I was going, a steering correction was impossible. I put my legs against the floor to brace myself so that I wouldn't fly over the wheel and into the windshield. I hit the trunk of a roughly 66-foot-tall (20-meter-tall) ash tree right on the edge of the forest, only a few feet off the road—it was terrible. My body was badly shaken, there was a crack in

Alfred Neubauer amongst his employees in Le Mans, 1952: He is considered the originator of the position of racing manager. "Don Alfredo" introduced a system of boards and flags on the side of the track with which he could give drivers instructions and let them know about the progress of the race.

the thigh of my right leg, and then it was quiet," said patient Rudolf Caracciola to the *Pirmasenser Zeitung* newspaper on May 30, 1952.

"Karratsch," as the Germans called him, was eliminated, and it would be a permanent departure. While the femoral neck fracture healed relatively quickly, Caracciola, one of the best drivers of all time, declared his retirement from motor sports after the mishap, his third serious accident.

24 HOURS OF LE MANS: A RESOUNDING SUCCESS

Over a bottle of wine in October 1922, three men decided to hold a 24-hour race to put the young technology of the automobile to a special test. The resulting race in Le Mans, launched in 1923, is considered one of the absolute highlights of the annual racing season. Emile Coquille, responsible for importing British Rudgerims, Georges Durand, the General Secretary of the Automobile Club de l'Ouest, and Charles Faroux, Editor in Chief of the periodicals *L'Auto* and *La Vie Automobile*, could not have suspected what they had begun with this idea. The "Vingt-Quatre Heures" would become a legend that continues to this day.

Those who win there write automobile history—and get a powerful selling point. Therefore, Daimler-Benz put in consid-

erable effort to eliminate any risk for this race. "99 percent of a race can be won with preparation—luck only contributes one percent to victory," said Alfred Neubauer.

Three new cars were used in the race: Hermann Lang and Fritz Riess drove the car with vehicle identification number 00007/52 and start number 21; Karl Kling and Hans Klenk got the 00008/52 and start number 22; and Theo Helfrich and his co-driver Helmut Niedermayr were entrusted with the car with vehicle identification number 00009/52 and start number 20. Kling/Klenk dropped out around 12:30 at night due to a defect with the alternator; Lang/Riess won, with Helfrich/Niedermayr coming in second. Le Mans became a tremendous success— but to Daimler-Benz, it was absolutely clear that luck had also played a role. Five vehicles from Ferrari and one Gordini had attained faster lap times, but they dropped out or took too much time in the pits. The Talbot of French driver Pierre Levegh was ahead of the 300 SL up to the 23rd hour, but then started losing oil, finally resulting in a cracked connecting rod. Levegh, who had driven the 23 hours solo, was jotted down in

24-hour race of Le Mans on June 13 and 14, 1952: Mercedes scores a sensational double victory. Hermann Lang and Fritz Riess win ahead of Theo Helfrich and Helmut Niedermayr (start number 20). Karl Kling and Hans Klenk (22), on the other hand, are eliminated.

Mercedes leaves nothing to chance in Le Mans, traveling with around 100 employees, including 40 mechanics and two mobile workshops. One hour before the end, they are seven laps behind Pierre Levegh in the Talbot, before he drops out due to engine damage.

Neubauer's notebook after this performance; Neubauer would give him the chance to drive the 300 SLR in Le Mans in 1955.

GRAND PRIX ON THE NÜRBURGRING: A TOTAL TRIUMPH

In order to cut weight for the next challenge, Mercedes removed the heavy coupé bodies and mounted roadster paneling. The automakers from Unter-türkheim took four vehicles to the Grand Prix on the Nürburgring: vehicle identification number 00002/52, driven by Karl Kling, received start number 24. The coupé with ID 00006/52 was rebuilt for Theo Helfrich into a roadster with the number 23; the silver roadster was also repainted green around the headlight section. Helfrich took fourth place in the race. The winning car from Le Mans with vehicle identification number 00007/52 appeared as a roadster with the start number 21; Hermann Lang would also drive it to victory on the Nürburgring. Finally, Fritz Riess piloted a 300 SL with vehicle identification number 00009/52 which had been painted red around the headlights and bore the number 22. He reached third place in the overall ranking.

Nürburgring Anniversary Grand Prix for sports cars on August 3, 1952:
An open-top version of the 300 SL is used for the first time, painted green
around the headlights. Theo Helfrich, seen here talking to Alfred Neubauer,
comes in fourth.

Vehicle identification number 00002/52 caused some confusion, since the car with license number W59-4029 appeared in the documents twice: it had appeared with a compressor in the class up to an eight-liter displacement during the training for the big anniversary race on July 31. It should actually have raced with the start number 31—if it had turned out during training that the 300 SLK was faster than the 300 SL, Neubauer would have reserved start numbers 31, 32, and 33.

The 300 SL with vehicle identification number 00002/52 had been used as a training car at the Mille Miglia and had previously been on standby in Berne as a backup vehicle. When it was modified into a roadster, not only was a M 197 supercharged engine installed (it had its own code number), the wheelbase was also shortened to 87 inches (2200 millimeters) in order to improve handling on the Nürburgring.

Ultimately, however, the M 197 did not deliver the advantages that Head Engineer Rudolf Uhlenhaut and driver Karl Kling had hoped. Although the single-stage Roots compressor had an output of 230 metric HP at 6400 rpm (the torque simultaneously increased to 28.8 mkg at 4200 rpm), the 300 SLK was just as fast as its brothers with 175 metric HP. As a result, start numbers 31 through 33 did not compete in the class up to an eight-liter displacement, but rather the cars with naturally aspirated engines and start numbers 22 through 24.

There was no supercharged engine in Kling's car, either, just the normal engine with the three Solex carburetors. Kling was in the lead with the "short" roadster before he spun on an oil slick caused by a leak in one of his car's oil lines. He nonetheless remained in second place behind Hermann Lang, who was able to secure his second victory after Le Mans. The cars of Riess and Helfrich took places three and four, leading the press office to proudly announce on August 3: "The first race on German soil became a smashing success for the 300 SL. All four cars delivered a superior performance in front of the 250,000 spectators."

CARRERA PANAMERICANA: "LIKE A GRENADE GOING OFF"

At the end of 1952, an official announcement stated that every sporting goal had been reached and the 300 SL race cars would disappear from the racetracks. However, a request was then made by the Mexican Daimler-Benz representative office, supported by the American im-

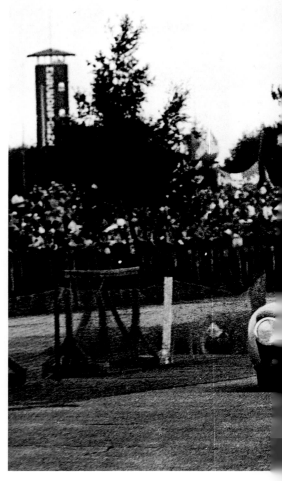

Quadruple triumph on the Nürburgring: Stuttgart-native Hermann Lang wins over a distance of 141.7 miles (228.1 kilometers). Today, the winning vehicle, which has been rebuilt back into a coupé, resides in the US.

porter: Daimler-Benz could still participate in the third iteration of the already legendary Carrera Panamericana.

This race was created in 1950 by the government in order to draw attention to the fact that there were now fully connected roads across Mexico—as well as to attract more wealthy US tourists to the country.

As an incentive, cash prizes amounting to about 35,000 dollars were offered—at the time, only in Indianapolis was there more money to be made in motor sports.

The Carrera Panamericana, named after the street, covered 1945 miles (3130 kilometers) over multiple stages from Ciudad Juarez, near the Mexican-American bor-

der, to El Ocotal, on the border with Guatemala. Should Daimler-Benz take up this immense challenge? The decision was reached quickly: three cars would be entered.

Vehicles with the following vehicle identification numbers were used: Coupé 00005/52, the car in which Rudolf

Caracciola had suffered his accident in Berne, was refurbished with a number of new parts for Hermann Lang and his co-driver Erwin Grupp. It was given the start number 3. Vehicle identification number 00008/52 was the reserve car on the Nürburgring—it bore the same license plate number as the vehicle with number 00002/52, which is one of the great unsolved mysteries in the history of this car. This roadster had been converted back into a coupé and was now handed over to Karl Kling and Hans Klenk with start number 4. The roadster with vehicle identification number 00009/52 kept its body and was piloted by the American John Fitch; he had impressed Alfred Neubauer with his driving skills in test drives on the Nürburgring. He was assigned the co-driver Eugen Geiger. The winning car from the Nürburgring served as the backup vehicle. This roadster, with vehicle identification number 00007/52, was driven by journalist

Günter Molter, who later acted as Press Officer for Daimler-Benz.

When reviewing the rules, they were surprised to discover that there was no dedicated 3-liter category in Mexico. Therefore, engineers increased the bore from 3.3 to 3.4 inches (85 to 86 millimeters)—the maximum, as more was not technically feasible. This resulted in a displacement of 3.1 liters and a maximum output of 177 metric HP, and thus a better torque curve, amounting to a maximum 58.2 pound-meters (26.4 kilogram-meters) at 4200 rpm.

The strongest competition consisted of various Ferraris and Lancia Aurelia B20 types. Ferrari entered four of the large 340 Mexico and 340 America models; there were also quite a few 212 Exports and a 250 S model for Giovanni Bracco and Gino Bronzoni. Lancia had also manned three B20 race cars with top drivers: Felice Bonetto, Giulio Casabianca, and Umberto Maglioli.

Neubauer decided not to go after Bracco and the other Ferrari teams on the first stages leading to Mexico City. He wanted to get his car to the capital city in one piece, then wage war in the high-speed stages. It was a clever decision, since the tires with the Nürburgring tread wore out sooner than even the worst pessimists had feared. What's more, drivers were already facing plenty of problems on the first section from Tuxtla Gutiérrez to Oaxaca: Hermann Lang hit a dog with his vehicle. The collision had bent the front section so badly that Lang feared damage to the steering system. Karl Kling was driving at about 137 mph (220 km/h) when a buzzard—or some sources say vulture—became unavoidable: "It hit like a grenade going off." The windshield had been cleanly pierced; a bloodied Hans Klenk sat next to Kling, while the mangled bird died in the rear. Klenk was patched up at the next pit stop and a safety grid made of iron struts was mounted in front of the windshield that evening. Despite this stop, Kling was in third place at the end of the stage; the other Mercedes cars followed in places seven and eight. In Mexico City, the two coupés were given the longer rear axle ratio which John Fitch had been driving with since the start. The stretch to Mexico City was full of curves, so the two coupés of Kling and Lang had a short transmission ratio for this route section; it allowed for better acceleration, but had a lower top speed. There were basically only long straightaways and relatively few curves from Mexico City to the finish line, so a long gear ratio was selected that enabled a higher final speed.

Legendary collision: At the 1952 Carrera Panamericana in Mexico, the 300 SL of Karl Kling and Hans Klenk collides with a bird of prey. The windshield bursts; Klenk is injured. He receives medical care at the next stop, while the front driver's section is equipped with a safety grid made of iron struts. Kling and Klenk win the race over the distance of 1945 miles (3130 kilometers), although the hot topic remains the spectacular accident. This contemporary drawing comes from painter and illustrator Hans Liska.

Considered the "Gentleman Racer," American John Fitch was the factory driver for Mercedes and took fifth place in the Mille Miglia with a 300 SL in 1955. It was won by Stirling Moss and Juan Manuel Fangio—also in a 300 SLR.

Before the final stretch, Fitch, Lang, and Kling were in places two through four, but Bracco led the pack in the Ferrari. The verdict came down during the seventh stage: Bracco dropped out with differential damage and two broken valve shafts. John Fitch had been disqualified shortly after the start in Parral. About a thousand feet (a few hundred meters) off the starting line, the American got the feeling that the steering and front suspension were not quite set correctly, so he turned around to have the car checked again. However, the rules clearly stated that repair work was not permitted during the race, which lead to the disqualification.

Despite tremendous efforts on the part of Neubauer to have his two remaining drivers, now safely in the lead, drive their coupés a little more carefully, Kling and Lang raced with unbridled spirit. Neubauer, who had chartered a Douglas DC-3 in order to monitor from the air, had a difficult time following the cars even in the plane, at least according to his memoirs. Kling reached top speeds of up to 155 mph (250 km/h) on the rural Mexican roads and interstates.

In Ciudad Juarez, the double victory for Mercedes was ensured: Karl Kling, along with Hans Klenk, won with an average speed of 102.3 mph (164.7 km/h), beating out Hermann Lang and Erwin Grupp.

The worst catastrophe in motor sports history:
Going more than 124 mph (200 km/h), Pierre Levegh
tries to swerve his 300 SLR out of the way of the British
Lance Macklin's surprising lane-change, and grazes his
Austin-Healey 100. Levegh's car explodes and flings
burning detritus into the crowd of spectators.

84 people die at the "Le Mans Disaster"—
in part because the fire fighters do not know
how to extinguish the burning magnesium
chassis of the 300 SLR. The race is not canceled.
As a consequence, Mercedes withdraws from
motor sports for almost 30 years.

It was an unprecedented triumph: Of the 92 cars that started, only 39 reached the finish line. Kling broke every course record, undercutting Taruffi's old record time by 17 percent. His winning time was 18:51.19 hours. It is no wonder that the press reports were enthusiastic. But that is not what pleased the finance executives at Daimler-Benz most; as stated in the newspaper *Die Welt* on 1952-12-13: "Mexico wants to drive Mercedes—in the week after the victory, more than 400 orders for the Type 300 were received, despite the price tag there of more than 115,000 pesos (about 57,000 German marks)."

1955: THE TRAGEDY OF LE MANS

It happened on June 11, 1955 in Le Mans. Mercedes started with three cars, driven by Juan Manuel Fangio, the young Stirling Moss, and Pierre Levegh, along with their respective "co-pilots." This was the same Pierre Levegh who had drawn attention at the same site in 1952 with his impressive solo driving.

After forgoing participation in sports car races in favor of Formula One in 1953 and 1954, Mercedes was back on the starting line in 1955 with a slightly modified W 196. It had won eleven races in Formula One, as well as two world championship titles.

In lap 35, on the home stretch, Levegh's vehicle collided with another vehicle and flipped over. Burning debris flew into the stands at high velocity. The driver and 83 spectators died in the tragedy; 100 more were seriously injured.

After the catastrophe of Le Mans, Daimler-Benz intended to quit motor sports immediately. However, Alfred Neubauer was able to convince the board members to at least secure the overall world championship title before their retirement—which is exactly what happened when Stirling Moss won the Targa Florio.

After 1955, the 300 SL was still used in races by private drivers on occasion. The American Chuck Porter achieved a few notable results in his SL with a modified body and engine.

Relatives in spirit: Mercedes has produced the current SL of the R 231 series since 2012.
It carries the genes of the Type 300 SL, W 194.

THE SL LEGACY

On all the sports cars that have try to keep up the legacy of the Gullwing

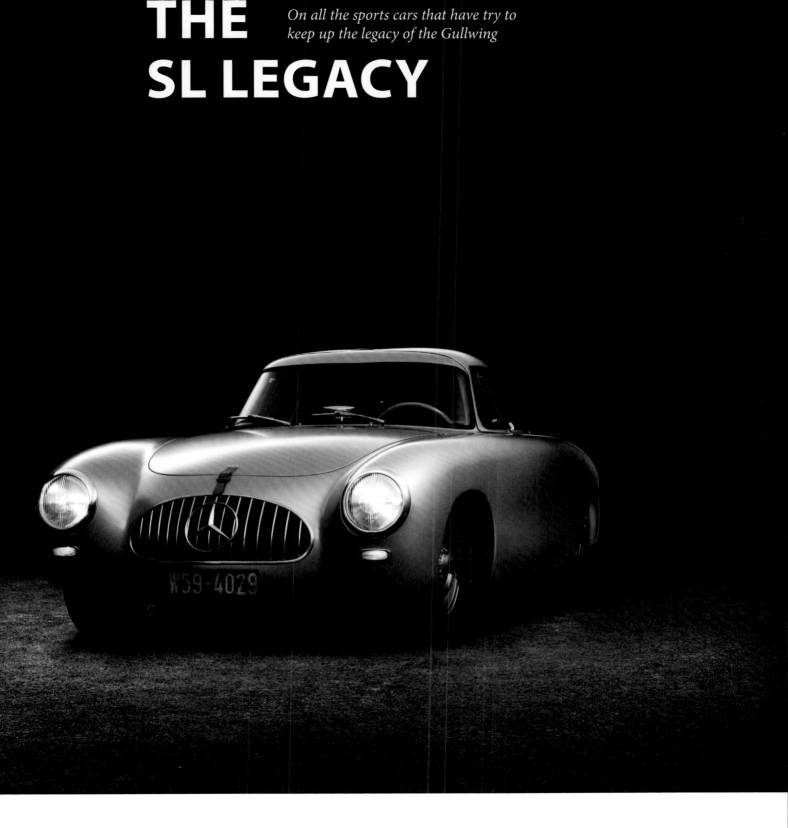

If we continue the "live fast, die young" idea from the previous chapter, you could say that, with regard to the reception of the 300 SL, it has definitely had a life after death. By their very nature, its successors inherited a difficult legacy—but they also did their part to keep the mythos alive.

LITTLE BROTHER, BIG SUCCESS

The latter is also true of the car's "little brother." The 190 SL was presented together with the 300 SL at the International Motor Sports Show in New York in February 1954. It quickly turned out to be the dream sports car for those who could not afford the expensive Gullwing. At about 17,000 German marks, the 190 SL was approximately 12,000 German marks cheaper than the 300 SL.

The family resemblance can be seen in the Mercedes star. Daimler Motoren Gesellschaft applied for a design patent for the three-pointed star on June 24, 1909. After the merger with Benz & Cie. in 1926, the logos also merged: Daimler contributed the star, Benz the laurel wreath. This signet hung proudly on the hood in 3D until the SL family appeared on the

Little brother: The 190 SL, known internally as
the W 121 B II, was marketed by Mercedes-Benz
as a "touring sports car."

The successor to both the 190 SL
and 300 SL: the W 113 series

Nicknamed the Pagoda SL, the W 113 was
built from 1963 to 1971 and offered as the
230 SL, 250 SL, and 280 SL.

The SL of the R 107 series was launched in 1971 and held on until 1989. The responsible designer: Friedrich Geiger, who had previously developed the original 300 SL.

scene. Its members now wore the star in the center of the radiator grill.

The 190 SL was powered by a 1.9-liter four-cylinder engine with 105 metric HP, giving it a top speed of 106 mph (171 km/h). This made it one of the fastest touring sports cars of its time. Meanwhile, the Swiss magazine *Automobil Revue* had this to say in November 1956: "Despite its high performance, the 190 SL is not a real sports car. Instead, it is a straightforward, serious touring car with all four of its tires firmly on the ground, so to speak. Thanks to its exemplary driving characteristics, it is one of the few vehicle types with which you can reach maximum average speeds in complete safety, without rushing, and with full consideration to other cars on the road."

With respect to legend status, the 190 SL definitely cannot keep up with the 300 SL. However, the first open-top series-production sports car of the SL family became a real sales success. Between 1955 and 1963, 25,881 units of the 190 SL were built.

Mercedes-Benz sold more than two hundred thousand
units of the R 129 series from 1989 to 2001.

SAFELY SWINGING INTO THE SIXTIES

Swinging sixties and safety? At first glance, the two concepts
might not seem to go together. However, the number of vehicles increased rapidly during this period. In Germany alone,
the Federal Motor Transport Authority saw the number of
passenger cars double from 4.5 to more than 9 million between 1960 and 1965. Naturally, the number of traffic accidents also rose at the same time. The 230 SL (1963–1971)
sought to counter this trend with extensive safety measures,
such as crumple zones and an interior that eliminated any
dangerous edges. At the same time, the successor of the 190 SL
and 300 SL exuded the appropriate amount of ease and elegance for the zeitgeist. Its nickname, the "Pagoda," was coined
because of its concave roof shape. The W 113 series was round-

The 300 SL 24 was on the market from 1989 to 1993. The six-cylinder engine output 231 metric HP and reached a top speed of 149 mph (240 km/h).

ed out with the 250 SL and 280 SL types and brought the total to 48,912 units.

AN EDGY BESTSELLER

Who says "die young"? The next member of the 300 SL family tree, the direct descendant of the Pagoda, made it to the age of majority. The R 107 was built for 18 years (1971–1989)—practi-

cally an eternity in car years. It underwent intensive model updates during this time. First, the 3.5-liter eight-cylinder engine, introduced two years prior, packed 200 metric HP under the large hood. Later, a 2.8-liter six-cylinder as well as a V8 engine with an enlarged five-liter displacement were added.

The R 107 initiated a paradigm shift with its exterior design, featuring a lightweight wedge shape, broad-band headlights,

The SL class is continued by the R 230 in 2001. The convertible offers a folding hardtop made of aluminum which can be stowed in the trunk using an electrohydraulic system.

and typical fluted side panels. As a whole, it had a much edgier appearance than its predecessors. This did not diminish its popularity: in total, 237,287 units were produced.

TAKING DESCENDANTS INTO NEW TERRITORY

The success story was continued by the descendents of the 300 SL. For example, take the R 129, built between 1989 and 2001 with a total of 204,940 units. A twelve-cylinder engine was used for the first time here, and the first official AMG versions of it were produced, i.e. high-performance vehicles developed by Mercedes subsidiary AMG. Or the R 230 (2001–2012), also equipped with the latest technology, which won over 169,434 buyers. Or the SLR McLaren (2003–2009), of which 2,100 units were built.

With acceleration up to 62 mph (100 km/h) in 3.8 seconds and a top speed of 209 mph (337 km/h), it ventured into new territory.

The Mercedes-Benz SLS AMG (SLS stands for "Sport, Light, Super") brought it full circle, although development naturally carried on. When it was presented at the IAA in 2009, you could finally say: "The Gullwing is back." The vehicle, developed and built by AMG, was the first Mercedes Gullwing since 1957. And finally, the SLS AMG Electric Drive has offered an electric variant since 2013. Neon yellow on the outside, 750 metric HP on the inside—making it the most powerful electric sports car of its time. The family saga continues…

Super sports car: The Mercedes-Benz SLR McLaren is produced from 2003 to 2009 in England. The butterfly doors and side vent openings are reminiscent of the Uhlenhaut Coupé. It starts at 476,000 euros.

The future starts earlier than expected: In 2013, Mercedes presents the SLS AMG Coupé Electric Drive. With a top speed of 155 mph (250 km/h), and it becomes the fastest electrically driven series production vehicle in the world. It is listed at 416,500 euros.

The Mercedes-Benz SLS AMG is the first series production vehicle from the Stuttgart automaker since the Uhlenhaut Coupé to offer gull-wing doors. Produced from 2009 until 2014, the eight-cylinder engine delivers 571 metric HP. It costs 225,505 euros.

Perfect light for practically perfect vehicles: René Staud (left) achieves the optimal conditions for fascinating shots with his patented Magicflash® lighting technology.

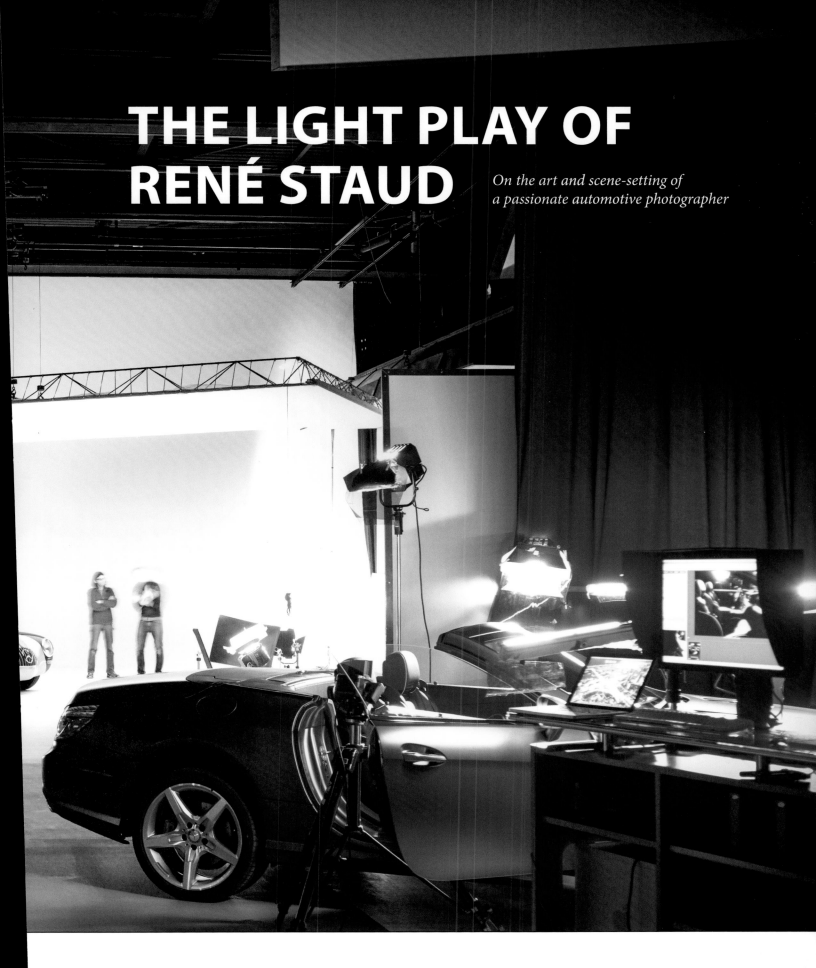

THE LIGHT PLAY OF
RENÉ STAUD

*On the art and scene-setting of
a passionate automotive photographer*

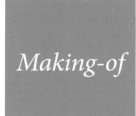
The viewer is inescapably drawn into his images. The skilled interplay of light and shadow which is produced by the Magicflash® lighting system he developed himself lets the surface of automobiles shine in perfect splendor. As a result, he is one of the most sought-after automotive photographers and considered one of the most innovative in the industry. We are talking about René Staud.

Staud has been devoted to the mesmerizing SL for more than three decades. The portfolio of the "master of light" from Leonberg includes high-quality prints, calendars, and books. All the products—including bestseller *The Mercedes-Benz 300 SL Book* published by teNeues—exude the photographer's passion for the cult automobile.

THE STARGAZER

From the beginning, Staud's automobile photography has been connected with the name Mercedes. The photographer remembers: "Why are cars always photographed in the countryside? I asked this question in early 1982, when I had just become the proud owner of a Mercedes-Benz and was flipping through the vehicle's catalog." The only problem: the lighting technology of his studio was not sufficient for photographing objects as large as a car, at least not to Staud's standards. He adapted his experiences from photographing jewelry and writing instru-

ments, he tinkered, he experimented—using vehicles from Mercedes, too—and the result was his own lighting system with gigantic softboxes. It allows Staud to interpret the contours of automobiles his own way—and not just those cars with the star. The segmentation in the Magicflash box enables control over individual lamps, generating an interesting gradient and achieving even better finish results.

A PERFECTLY SET SCENE

The softboxes can also be used as part of the scene, as in the shot on page 34 of this book. Speaking of scene-setting, René Staud is also skilled at creating photographic illusions. The photo on page 66 gives the impression that the vehicle is actually hanging on the wall. The making-of image on the right shows how it was done.

Media company *Motor Presse Stuttgart* raves: "René Staud is a brilliant photographer and a true master of his profession. His works of art are finely balanced compositions of light and color given shape by photoflash. His inspired pictures of breathtaking body design have set milestones in modern automobile photography. Elegance and refinement of style and execution characterize his unique type of photography: engineering in a most aesthetic form bathed with great sensitivity in a new light."

Trickery is okay: The trick to the hanging 300 SL on page 66 is that everything is set on the ground.

MERCEDES-BENZ 300 SL
LIVE & ON SITE

MERCEDES-BENZ MUSEUM

The museum, opened in 2006, is a must-see attraction—even for its dramatic, futuristic design, created by Dutch architectural firm UNStudio. The 177,604-square-foot (16,500-square-meter) space is the most-visited museum in Stuttgart. It takes visitors on a trip through more than 130 years of automotive history. Among the 160 vehicles on display, there are 300 SL models next to other rarities in the "Mythos 4" room—and "Legends 4" holds the original vehicle with which Kling and Klenk went on to win the Carrera Panamericana following the legendary vulture nosedive into the windshield. There are also special exhibitions that change on a regular basis.
Mercedesstrasse 100, 70372 Stuttgart, Germany, Phone +49 711 17 30 000, Tues–Sun 9 a.m.–6 p.m.; www.mercedes-benz.com/museum

TECHNIK MUSEUM SINSHEIM

The Technik Museum Sinsheim technology museum is only one hour from Stuttgart by car. In addition to steam engines and other curiosities, it also offers an exciting transportation collection, from the nostalgic bicycle to the world-record Blue Flame car to the supersonic plane. One of the highlights is the largest permanent Formula 1 exhibition in Europe. Several 300 SL cars also stand among the 300 classic cars in the collection.
Museumsplatz, 74889 Sinsheim, Germany, Phone +49 7261 92 990, open daily, 9 a.m.–6 p.m. (Sat/Sun until 7 p.m.); www.sinsheim.technik-museum.de

AUTOSAMMLUNG STEIM

The Autosammlung Steim car collection also resides in Baden-Wuerttemberg. In Schramberg in the Black Forest, the 32,292-square-foot (3000-square-meter) exhibition space holds

Time Travel

more than 100 vehicles which represent more than 100 years of automobile history. They come from the private collection of entrepreneur Dr.-Ing. (Doctor of Engineering) Hans-Jochem Steim, and are supplemented by loaned exhibits. This collection includes a 1955 300 SL coupé, a 1956 190 SL roadster in original condition, as well as a 300 SL roadster from 1958.
Göttelbachstrasse 49, 78713 Schramberg, Germany, Phone +49 7422 97 90 901, Summer: Tues–Sun 10 a.m.–6 p.m., Autumn: Tues–Sun 10 a.m.–5 p.m., Winter: Sat/Sun 10 a.m.–5p.m.; www.autosammlung-steim.de

EFA—MOBILE AGE

The history of the automobile in Germany during the 20th century is the theme of the "EFA—Mobile Age" exhibit in Amerang in the Chiemgau area of Bavaria. What makes the museum special is the access it gives you to every single one of the cultural and historical aspects of the automobile phenomenon. The collection includes more than 250 historical vehicles and innumerable items from the history of automobile culture. The museum promises "absolute legends that have shaped entire epochs." Of course, it would not be complete without a Gullwing from 1955.
Wasserburger Strasse 38, 83123 Amerang, Germany, Phone +49 8075 81 41, Thurs–Sun 10 a.m.–6 p.m. (open from March–November); www.efa-mobile-zeiten.de

CITÉ DE L'AUTOMOBILE

In an exhibition space of 269,098 square feet (25,000 square meters), the Cité de l'Automobile houses the largest automobile collection in the world. The inventory of the museum, located in the Alsatian town of Mulhouse, is based on the famed Schlumpf collection. Brothers Hans and Fritz Schlumpf had accumulated one of the greatest automobile collections, mostly in the 1960s; however, their passion was ultimately the ruin of their textile factory. Its former rooms house the museum today. A white 300 SL coupé from 1955 is in illustrious company there.
17 rue de la Mertzau, 68100 Mulhouse, France, Phone +33 3 89 33 23 23; Visiting hours vary and can be found on the museum's website: www.citedelautomobile.com/de

Photo: The "Mythos 7" area in the Mercedes-Benz Museum in Stuttgart celebrates a successful motor sports history.

Imprint

© **2022 teNeues Verlag GmbH**
All rights reserved

Published by Axel Nowak

Text: Jürgen Lewandowski
Design and layout: Eva Stadler
Image editing and captions: Axel Nowak
Image processing and proofs: Jens Grundei, teNeues Verlag
Production: Sandra Jansen-Dorn, teNeues Verlag
Translation, copyediting and typesetting: STAR Software,
Translation, Artwork, Recording GmbH
Proofreading: Stephanie Rebel, teNeues Verlag
Editorial coordination: Luisa Krause-Rossa, teNeues Verlag

ISBN 978-3-96171-413-1
Library of Congress Number: 2022942809

Printed in Slovakia by Neografia

Published by teNeues Publishing Group

teNeues Verlag GmbH
Ohmstraße 8a
86199 Augsburg, Germany

Düsseldorf Office
Waldenburger Str. 13
41564 Kaarst, Germany
Email: books@teneues.com

Augsburg/Munich Office
Ohmstraße 8a
86199 Augsburg, Germany
Email: books@teneues.com

Berlin Office
Lietzenburger Str. 53
10719 Berlin, Germany
Email: books@teneues.com

Press Department
Email: presse@teneues.com

teNeues Publishing Company
350 Seventh Avenue, Suite 301, New York,
NY 10001, USA
www.teneues.com

teNeues Publishing Group
Augsburg / München
Berlin
Düsseldorf
London
New York

teNeues